CARS TO REMEMBER

CARS TO REMEMBER

Thirty-seven Great Automobiles in Retrospect

Bill Neely and John Lamm
and the editors of **Motor Trend** Magazine

HENRY REGNERY COMPANY • CHICAGO

Library of Congress Cataloging in Publication Data

Neely, Bill.
    Cars to remember.

    1. Automobiles—Popular works.   I. Title.
TL146.5.N43   629.22'22   75-13234
ISBN: 0-8092-8241-0

Acknowledgments

We would like to acknowledge the assistance of the original coauthors of the *Motor Trend* articles adapted in this book: Kyle Given, John Christy, Eric Dahlquist, Wally Wyss, Karl Ludvigsen, Chris Packard, Ted West, Jack Woodard, David E. Davis, Jr., Steve Spence, Chuck Queener, and Carl Hungness.

All photographs courtesy Petersen Publishing Company

Copyright © 1975 by Bill Neely
All rights reserved
Published by Henry Regnery Company
                180 North Michigan Avenue
                Chicago, Illinois 60601
Manufactured in the United States of America
Library of Congress Catalog Card Number: 75-13234
International Standard Book Number: 0-8092-8241-0

Published simultaneously in Canada by
    Fitzhenry & Whiteside Limited
    150 Lesmill Road
    Don Mills, Ontario M3B 2T5
    Canada

Contents

Introduction:
"Classic" versus "Special Interest"

Any car manufactured prior to January 1, 1916, is generally termed a horseless carriage; "classic," with some exceptions, refers to large, powerful, luxury automobiles manufactured between 1925 and 1942. But special-interest cars are not so easily defined.

Classic cars have been defined as distinctive cars manufactured with quality materials and superb craftsmanship. They are practical cars, outstanding in appearance, performance, dependability, and utilitarian value, generally manufactured during the twenties or thirties—expensive in price and produced in limited numbers.

If the true classic must meet and fulfill each listed adjective, it is apparent that comparatively few cars will achieve that golden status. Those cars meeting some of the rigid requirements that guarantee a model fame are of "special interest."

There is as much distinction between the special-interest car and the ordinary car as between the special-interest car and the classic. Perhaps the best way to illustrate the difference is to compare an ordinary car with a special-interest car of the same make. Let us choose a two-door sedan manufactured in the mid-thirties. In all probability, it would not be wanted by enthusiasts unless its condition was so remarkable that it amounted to a showpiece. Condition is therefore a feature that may be considered in determining whether a car is of special interest. If a car cannot be used daily because of an inherent mechanical defect, its value is generally lower than the value of a comparable car that can be used for daily transportation.

However, condition is not the only determining factor. If the same two-passenger coupe model had side mounts, it would be of slightly more value and more popular with collectors.

And had the two-door coupe been a four-door convertible sedan of the same make and year, a car much more pleasing in appearance, it would truly be a special-interest car.

In other words, the degree of distinction affects the degree of special interest. This in turn directly affects the financial value of the car. Rarity, demand, condition, and performance are all important considerations.

Special-interest cars may be distinctive in very different ways. Mechanical innovation, mechanical oddity, unusual construction, and many other factors may enable a car to qualify. A car may even be of special interest because it is homely. This is true of the 1935 Hupmobile coupe; the car was downright homely and unusual and individual solely for that reason.

Mechanical oddity is as important as anything else. Three-wheel cars such as the Morgan, the prewar Bantam and Austins are of special interest. So are those cars equipped with unusual bodies, such as the Ford Sportsman and the Kaiser Traveler (the station wagon that looked like a sedan). An unusual number of features such as verified and/or authenticated prior history, age novelty, automotive innovation, and simple popularity may also raise a car to the level of special interest.

Close adherence to the foregoing complete definition means due consideration of every element and feature. It is true that any adjective or verb means different things to different people. An actress may be beautiful in the eyes of one fan, homely in the eyes of another. The same is true of appearance in connection with an automobile. A car that performs well for one person may be sluggish and trucklike according to the standards of another. But a car must be distinctive in the eyes of many before it qualifies as "special interest." The cars celebrated on the following pages truly qualify.

7

1957 Austin-Healey 100-Six

1957 AUSTIN-HEALEY 100-SIX

Engine Type: overhead valve in-line 6-cylinder

Displacement: 2.6 liters (158.6 cubic inches)

Horsepower: 102

Transmission: 4-speed manual

Wheelbase: 92 inches

Overall Length: 157.5 inches

Overall Height: 49 inches

Overall Width: 60.5 inches

Restoration is the one word that keeps many of us from being classic car collectors. There are countless opportunities to *purchase* a semi-classic car; it is the idea of *restoring* it that keeps most people at arm's length. The following is an account of former *Motor Trend* Associate Editor Kyle Given's restoration of a 1957 Austin-Healy:

I paid a hundred and fifty bucks for it in January 1973. I bought it from Bill Russom who had just taken the art director's job at *Hot Rod* magazine; I suppose he didn't want to confuse anybody.

I went to pick it up with Jim Weiser, neighbor and pal, who sizes up investments with all the heartfelt enthusiasm and personal involvement of a sadder-but-wiser computer memory bank. Weiser, too, had purchased a flogged Healey for $150 a month earlier. A '62 3000 Mark 1. His would prove to be a better buy.

"I smell gasoline," Weiser snickered as we stumbled through the graffiti and clutter of Russom's carport the afternoon we went down to Santa Monica to pick up my '57 100-Six. I had never seen it before, having trusted to descriptions of its worth by Russom.

"What can you lose, it's only a hun and a half," I recalled Russom shrugging as Weiser spotted the car in a far corner and we began to

walk toward it. One of its decrepit Dunlops was flat. The battery was dead. The faded and torn top was half-drawn over the interior, which I could see by peering through the cracked, crazed Plexiglas side curtains. It was littered with beer cans, old rags, yellowing sports sections and parts that had fallen off the car. Like the front bumper.

The once-deep metallic blue paint was scarred, chipped, patched by sporadic blotches of green stuff and spray-can primer, and was discolored to a vaguely purplish shade.

The body was indescribable. In an attempt to create some sort of analytical order toward the, uh, coachwork, I took a tape out of my pocket and tried to find at least one square yard of sheet metal that wasn't dented, ripped, or gouged. The hood, the "bonnet," passed. But one rocker panel was rusted through and the other would never qualify for Blue Cross. Indeed, what could I lose?

We transfer-tubed some air into the tire, muscled the car out of the garage and down a hill. It caught in third gear and that's the way Weiser drove it out the San Diego Freeway to Barri's Auto Works on Ventura Boulevard in the Valley. In third gear—because the clutch slave cylinder was shot. At about 1500 rpm—because the overdrive was out and the valves were, ah, sticking?

During the ride out there, I fulminated that on a 1–10 scale of prudent financial incidence, this one seemed to rate right at lunacy. Still, we felt, the theory was in the ballpark.

The idea was (and remains) to get into a "sort-of" unique car for very low bucks, drive it during its economical restoration, and then unload it for a bundle more than the total investment. Our goal was to aim at a $1500 ceiling, but not to be outraged if it wrapped at a couple thou. (Have some fun, make a buck.)

We even thought of a name for the as-yet-unborn movement: Cult Cars—those sporty "kind-of" cars from the late forties, fifties, and early sixties that have retained a surprising continuation of affectionate acceptance from a few people who should know a whole lot better. Cult Cars don't have to be very good cars even

1957 Austin-Healey 100-six
Owner: Kyle Given   Photographed for *Motor Trend* by John Lamm

WHAT IT COST TO RESTORE 1957 AUSTIN-HEALEY 100-SIX

Job Description	Parts	Labor	Total
Purchase	150.00		150.00
Bodywork and paint, replacement of front and rear bumpers and guards	136.00	469.00	605.00
Cost to get car running	37.15	110.00	147.15
Rebuilding cooling system	74.30	35.00	109.30
The horn	55.00	30.00	85.00
Replacement of rod bearings, oil pressure relief valve	36.10	45.00	81.10
Windshield	67.50		67.50
Delco battery	49.50		49.50
Fuel, water and oil gauges, miscellaneous mechanical work (emergency brake, bulbs, nuts, etc.)	43.50	45.00	88.50
Speedometer	24.85	5.00	29.85
Rebuilding heater and controls	9.50	20.00	29.50
Tuning and tightening rear suspension		29.50	29.50
Rebuilding clutch/brake slave cylinders	6.25	15.00	21.25
Rebuilding exhaust system	6.10	15.00	21.10
Lube/oil change/filter	9.90	5.00	14.90
Tonneau and snaps	6.72	68.00	74.72
Reupholstering top of dash		35.00	35.00
Body detailing (fender beading, antenna, rear mirror)	31.20	34.84	66.04
Mr. V.P. Haan's Big Kid's Candy Store Goodies	31.90		31.90
Pirelli F85 x 15 x 5½ Radials @ $57.50 each	230.00		230.00
5½-inch rims, 72-Spoke Triumph TR-6 Wheels @ $103.24 each	413.00		413.00
Michelin tubes and tire busting, wheel balancing	30.40	6.00	36.40
Miscellaneous (license, registration, various oddiments)	110.89	110.89	221.79
TOTAL	**$1559.76**	**$1078.23**	**$2637.99**

when compared against the standards of their time.

Take the middle-fifties Porsche Speedsters. A couple of years ago you could buy a nice Speedster for around $1000. Now they're going for a minimum of $3000, with some selling for $6000. They are ugly. They're uncomfortable and there isn't a new Superbug around that can't blow the doors off a stock one. Clearly, they are not a desirable car. But they are.

As cars, Cult Cars have only a few things going for them. Cult Cars are:

1. Getting scarce,
2. Capable of turning heads,
3. (Somehow) fun,
4. Easily restorable at this time.

That parts are still available, that they are not subject to smog and safety legislation and subsequently keep a tune and give good gas mileage does not exactly hurt the equation.

Weiser and I share another attitude—we'll be damned if we'll pay $6000 for a 1957 automobile. We began looking around, talking to guys, trying to determine where the Cult Car thing was going to happen next. It appeared that the Jaguar XK-120 roadsters and coupes would follow the Speedsters, because after all there are only so many middle-fifties Porsches floating around.

Well, fans, we were a little timid about the Jaguar thing. When we first started looking at them, the prices ranged from a grotty $600 to $1500 for cream puffs of almost lyrical condition. Try to touch one now for less than $1,500. Lightning.

"What's the most beautiful English sports car ever made?" Weiser asked one moody afternoon.

"What are six-cylinder Healeys selling for?" I asked. (The fours, though better proportioned, are a hassle to drive.)

"Around $150," Weiser replied.

Which brings us full-circle to that 110-degree day on the San Diego Freeway in a sixteen-year-old Healey that is running terribly and which, it turns out, has the heater full-on. The control knob was stuck.

Frank Godbille is the proprietor of Barri's Auto Works. He reveres Jaguars, admits that MGs are slightly interesting historically and endures Healeys. He is the guy to go see about restoring your old imported sports clunker in the Los Angeles area. His shop does it all, from mechanical work, to farming out upholstery, to body and paint. But don't cross him and don't confuse him. Tell him how much you want to spend and leave him alone.

There was only one time during the roughly six months that the car remained on his premises that Frank asked my advice. "What color should we paint it?" he asked.

"Oh, I don't know," I said. "I was thinking of something kind of subtle like a discreet beige,

Concours d'Elégance originality. The cars can be put back into original shape easily enough, but there is none of that slavish devotion to *pur sang* condition crap that warps the attitudes of *Concours* buffs. Cars are to be enjoyed. Not suffered. Some of the better restored Porsche Speedsters running around L.A., for instance, have recent six-cylinder engine swaps and bigger rubber. The interiors are fitted with more comfortable seats and good sound systems.

In keeping with that attitude, I did one thing that was at once the smartest and the dumbest move of the entire Healey project. I wanted big Pirelli radials on it. (Nothing improves a car's behavior as much as bigger, better tires, and Pirellis are the best.) To accommodate the bigger tires, I needed wide-rimmed wheels, and I wanted them to be wire wheels. Well, the next expenditure was $643 worth of better handling, riding, and looks. It's the single biggest improvement made on the car and it's also the most expensive.

One other thing I learned that might save some of the more mechanically inclined Cult Car guys a buck or two in repairs is the incredible list of factory repair manuals available through Classic Car Books (3106/Y9 West Lake Street, Minneapolis, Minn. 55416). They fixed me up with an "Austin-Healey 100-Six and 3000 Workshop Manual" and a "Healey Owners Handbook," either of which tells (and shows) just about everything you need to know to do your own work on a similar project car. (I also got an interesting book about the history of the cars, "Healeys and Austin-Healeys," crammed full of pictures and racing lore, which bores me to sleep, but is factual and informative.) It doesn't seem to matter what kind of old sports clunk you have, Classic Car Books has a factory repair manual for it. That is no small item.

something with a little class." It came from the spray booth—burgundy. (I think burgundy has class, don't you, Frank?)

Cult Car guys are not slaves to the idea of

1955 Packard Caribbean

1955 PACKARD CARIBBEAN

Engine Type: overhead valve V-8
Displacement: 352 cubic inches (5.7 liters)
Horsepower: 275
Transmission: 2-speed automatic
Wheelbase: 127 inches
Overall Length: 217 inches
Overall Height: 62 inches (top up)
Overall Width: 78 inches

They stopped making Packards, real Packards, in October of 1956. They moved the Packard assembly line from Detroit to South Bend, Indiana, where the newly merged Studebaker-Packard Corporation had begun by building Conestoga wagons in the mid-1800s. After October of '56 Packards "didn't look right. All they did was take a Hawk and hang some different chrome on it," according to Don Schmid, the former Wichita Packard dealer who now sells Dodges on the same site.

The '55 Caribbean was the last glamorous

gasp from Packard. And it was a helluva car, grotesque (in retrospect) paint schematics and anal-compulsive rear-end styling treatments to the contrary.

For its time it was a large car. With a wheelbase of 127 inches and an overall length of 217.4 inches, it had a lot of overhanging sheet metal, mostly toward the rear, perhaps to balance the anchorlike 352 cu. in. V-8 in front. By current standards of luxury cars, it was a tidier exterior than many new Chevrolets.

If the Caribbean oozed a sort of Andy Warhol charm in terms of color, it still performed fairly well. This attribute was due in part to Packard's new-for-'55 "Torsion-Level Ride." More than twenty-six feet of full chassis length torsion bars and compensators kept the 8.00 x 15 rubber on the ground. An airbag leveler unit was an option on the other two full-sized Packards, the Patrician and the 400.

The 352 cu. in. V-8 was standard throughout the entire Packard line, multiplicity of engine sizes and performance options being a thing of the future for '55. But the Caribbean was a quasi-factory hot rod of sorts, because it came stock with dual 4-barrel carbs, and developed 15 more horsepower at 200 higher rpm than either the Patrician or the 400. The torque range was

RETROSPECT

1955 Packard Caribbean   Owner: Jamie Kay
Photographed for Motor Trend by Mike Salisbury

wider in the Caribbean, also, from 2400 to 3200 rpm and the delivery was at 355 foot-pounds.

For '55, all Packards came with a new 12-volt electrical system, the better to churn a full complement of power accessories; and all Packards had dual exhausts.

1940 Packard Station Wagon

1940 PACKARD STATION WAGON

Engine Type: L-head in-line 8-cylinder

Displacement: 356 cubic inches (5.8 liters)

Horsepower: 160

Transmission: 3-speed manual with overdrive

Wheelbase: 127 inches

Overall Length: 216 inches

Overall Height: 74 inches

Overall Width: 76 inches

Americans love station wagons, especially wooden ones. And this one is very special. The classic Packard grille leads the way for a long, appropriately aquiline, aristocratic nose—a prow that cleaves the air for a vast wooden box of a body. A body of ash and birch, about the same height as your average telephone booth. The 1940 Packard Station Wagon is a tall, handsome, *noblesse-oblige* kind of car from a time when terms like "upper crust" and "cafe society" were meaningful social indicators.

Packard was dying in 1940. The disease had been diagnosed as too narrow a range of models clustered in the high-priced bracket and the cure prescribed was the addition of a bunch of cheapy six-cylinder pseudo-Packards at the other end of the market scale. In 1938 they even cheapened the eight-cylinder cars, and in 1939 they dropped their twelve-cylinder model. But there were still a lot of Packard lovers out there in 1940, and the One-Sixty Super Eight Station Wagon was aimed at the old Packard status market—a nice car for nice wealthy people.

But this is no ordinary Packard station wagon. This is not the standard One-Ten or One-Twenty station wagon. This is probably the only station wagon ever built on the One-Sixty Super Eight chassis. This one has twin spare tires mounted in the front fenders. The crummy little Packard One-Ten only has one spare and it's mounted behind the front seat (if you can imagine). The One-Twenty carries a single outside spare mounted in the right front fender, at least, but it just doesn't make the same kind of statement. And the One-Sixty Super Eight has discreet little chrome messages mounted on the spare tire covers that say AIR CONDITIONED—a Packard first for 1940. Air conditioned! Most of the people in the United States have never even been in an air-conditioned building, for God's sake, and here you are in an air-conditioned automobile.

Sitting inside this Packard One-Sixty Super Eight Station Wagon is like sitting inside a prewar cabin cruiser—because of all the wood. On the *inside*. The side panels are birch plywood and the headliner is made of long curved strips of ash, about an inch wide, held in place by beautifully fitted ash crossmembers. The seats are very businesslike affairs, exposed steel tube frames with leatherette upholstery stretched over the same kind of springs used in the Packard sedans of the period.

The ride is boatlike, too. It's the classic American car ride that all us sports car people complained about in the years after World War II. With Safe-T-Flex suspension, it is absolutely smooth and soft with good directional stability, but a very tentative, pessimistic feeling going around corners. It does roll some. But back in 1940, America's overachievers had no interest in handling as we know it today. You drove fast on the straights and slowed down for the corners—a lot. The popular notion of a high-speed corner was executed in something like a

In Retrospect

1940 Packard Station Wagon   Owner: Harrah's Automobile Collection
Photographed for Motor Trend by John Lamm

Ford Tudor or five-window by spinning the rear wheels as you exited a right angle intersection in downtown Fort Wayne, Indiana, which allowed the rear end to swing wide in a kind of noisy first-gear dirt-tracking yaw. Ersatz, but gratifying. Nobody ever did that in a Packard.

Sitting behind the steering wheel is another exercise in nostalgia. The steering wheel is a large three-spoked device carved from a solid billet of pearlescent prewar plastic by elderly Polish craftsmen working in the old Packard plant on Detroit's East Grand Boulevard. It would look very much at home sticking out of one of those blond mahogany Telefunken radio/phonographs that were so big in the fifties.

The instrumentation is complete and self-explanatory, but the control knobs are something else altogether. These latter devices are all the same size and shape, all carved from the same solid billet of sturdy prewar plastic as the steering wheel, and all equally, inscrutably anonymous. Even the radio controls conceal their identity in marbled beige mufti. God help the novice One-Sixty Super Eight Packard Station Wagon driver if he needed the lights, heater, hand choke, cigarette lighter, or radio on short notice.

You reach over, switch on the radio (giving it about three minutes for the tubes to warm up) and you get Wee Bonnie Baker singing her popular rendition of "Oh, Johnny Oh!" backed up by Orrin Tucker's orchestra. "South of the Border" is also big, but war songs like "A Nightingale Sang In Berkeley Square" and "The Last Time I Saw Paris" are beginning to show up on the Hit Parade. Push KOWL and they interrupt the music to tell you that France has fallen.

But none of that heavy stuff made much difference to Mr. Solid Citizen Packard One-Sixty Super Eight Station Wagon Driver in those days. Smoothly, silently humming along the road in his big cream-colored boat-car, the Middle-American of that era didn't concern himself too much with what was happening Over There, wherever "Over There" might be. Nineteen-forty was America's last full year of innocence and America was enjoying the hell out of it.

Even Washington seemed pretty far away. The presidential race between FDR and Wendell Willkie was probably the hottest issue of the day. There was a lot of noise about Lend-Lease

and our nonviolent participation in the Battle of Britain, but the average guy wasn't too interested unless he worked the swing-shift at Lockheed making Hudson bombers for the R.A.F. In fact it wasn't too hard to find rather vocal German sympathizers among one's friends and neighbors at that early phase of World War II. Through Lend-Lease, and the burgeoning European hostilities, Packard was given one more chance to make it big.

The British had made a deal with the Ford Motor Company to produce the sensational Rolls-Royce aircraft engine that powered the Spitfires. Ford had done a lot of research and development in the production engineering area and appeared all set, when old Henry Ford—always a sort of muddled pacifist and now half nuts besides—pulled the rug out from under his son Edsel, as well as the British government, and welshed on the deal.

Because of that, the British switched to Packard and Packard found itself in a position to make quite a lot of money. It was the first of a number of important war materiel contracts handled by Packard in the Second World War, and the apparent mismanagement of the resulting profits is regarded by many old Detroit hands as a prime cause of the company's final undoing in the postwar years.

In the meantime, in spite of their financial woes, Packard was making the One-Sixty Super Eight Station Wagon—much more like a very expensive European luxury car than any contemporary American car in the Packard class. In order to own a car like this in 1940, you'd have arranged for Packard to sell you a Model 1803-160 chassis with full front-end sheet metal and ship it to the Hercules Body Company at 1501 W. Franklin Street in Evansville, Indiana. The running chassis would have cost you about $1,450 and the Hercules body perhaps another $3,500.

Your chassis would have had a wheelbase of 127 inches—front tread width 59 3/16, rear tread width 62 1/2. Packard literature of the period describes the frame as a "Tempered I-Beam X-Member." The Safe-T-Flex suspension consisted of coil springs in the front with lever-type shocks and an anti-sway bar, and semi-elliptic leaf springs at the rear with aircraft-type hydraulic shocks. Brakes were Packard servo-hydraulic twelve-inch drums at all four corners, with linings 2.25 inches wide. It had a three-speed manual transmission with column-

mounted shift lever, and Hotchkiss drive carried the power back to the Hypoid rear axle—which in itself was still new enough to rate special mention in the specifications—and a final drive ratio of 4.09. Packard's Econo-Drive, an overdrive with free wheeling, was optional at extra cost. Tires were 7.00 x 16 with the widest whitewalls you ever saw in your whole entire life.

The engine was a paragon of no-nonsense 1940 automotive virtue. It was a straight eight with a 3 1/4-in. bore and a 4 5/8-in. stroke that multiplied out to a displacement of 356 cubic inches. It was a nice simple flat head—none of your noisy overhead cams or valves or pushrods or any of that monkey-motion. No sir. An L-head. Fundamental automotive truth. It breathed out 160 horsepower at 3,500 rpm and featured a modern-as-tomorrow no-lead or low-lead compression ratio of 6.45-1. Heady stuff.

The engine is virtually silent. Not because there are great wads of fibrous matting and clots of rubber stuffed in between you and it, but

because it's a quiet engine. With no complicated valve gear and hardly any engine-driven accessories, it just doesn't make any noise.

The Hercules people clothed all this mechanical conservatism in a wooden body that would make the cabinets in your house look like packing cases—beautiful joints, no sharp edges, piano hinges wherever one panel must swing away from another (yes, piano hinges). The floor was virtually flat and covered with nice, sensible rubber mat. There were no vent-windows in the front, but the rearmost side windows could slide open for half their length. The back window flipped upward and could be snap-locked into position and the tailgate folded flat, strong enough to support extra cargo when necessary. The whole package weighed 3,855 lbs. when it rolled out the door in Evansville.

The basic interior configuration for all Packard wagons was a 3-2-3 seating arrangement, not unlike Chevrolet's present-day Suburban Carry-all. This layout provided an aisle from the right-hand rear door to the rearmost seat. However, it was popular to eliminate the two-passenger second seat and move the third seat forward, which provided more luggage space and still accommodated a total of six adults—plenty for most families.

What's most impressive is the Packard's quiet comfort. It didn't rattle and bang like most contemporary wagons. Oh, it creaked a little, but what yacht doesn't?

The wagon in Harrah's Automobile Collection is so nice that it's popular with the boss and others as a regular business vehicle. As a result, it offers a couple of refinements the elderly Polish craftsmen on East Grand Boulevard never thought of. The air conditioning has been rerouted to blow cool air from beneath the dash instead of its 1940 location behind the rear seat, and a modern compressor has replaced the old Packard unit up front. There's a roll bar hidden in the woodwork behind the rear doors, and the rear suspension has been updated with the addition of a Delco load-leveling device. But like everything else about the cars in Harrah's incredible, immaculate collection, even these modifications seem logical and right and one accepts them in the spirit in which they were intended.

The Packard One-Sixty Super Eight Station Wagon actually started life as two Packards. One was a 1940 Packard One-Sixty Super Eight Touring Sedan and the other was a One-Twenty station wagon of similar vintage. The Hercules body was duplicated by the Harrah organization's own craftsmen, using as many odds and ends of hardware and equipment as could be saved from the old wagon, while most of the original Packard components came intact from the big Super Eight sedan.

However it came about, the result is a glorious statement of what the good life was like back in antebellum 1940. Without arrogance, without accusation, the old Packard One-Sixty Super Eight Wagon makes it pretty clear that there hasn't been much automotive progress really since 1940.

1943 Willys Jeep

1943 WILLYS JEEP

Engine Type: L-head in-line 4-cylinder

Displacement: 134.2 cubic inches (2.2 liters)

Horsepower: 54

Transmission: 3-speed manual

Wheelbase: 80 inches

Overall Length: 131 inches

Overall Height: 72 inches

Overall Width: 62 inches

There is simply no doubt at all about who owns the Jeep trademark today—the American Motors Corporation. They possess the name outright and protect it with the ferocity of a mother grizzly watching over a single cub.

It is a valuable property, that trademark, because it represents a vehicle that will rank in history alongside the Model T. Henry Ford's basic transportation package lasted through a model run of eighteen years, from 1909 to 1927 during which some fifteen million were built. The basic Jeep package—truck, quarter-ton, Command Reconnaissance, GP—has lasted for over thirty years, albeit with a couple of face lifts and several powerplant changes. The Model T put a nation on wheels and helped begin the automobile industry as we know it today. The ubiquitous Jeep helped win the biggest war in history and later put a world on wheels, having been scattered across the globe wherever World War II Allied military forces had fought or been stationed. Rugged, spartan, uncomfortable and utterly simple, it was also indestructible, even in the hands of the totally untrained indigenous populations of the undeveloped lands where untold thousands were dumped when hostilities ended.

Perhaps the most interesting thing about the Jeep is that it was not the invention or even the concept of one individual or even one firm. It was probably the last example of inter-corporate cooperation (though possibly somewhat forced) and quite probably a number of federal trade and antitrust laws were contravened, if not outrightly flouted, in the process. As World War II approached and the nation began its belated re-armament, a long-standing military dream, requirement if you will, surfaced—a light, general purpose scout car. The lightest thing around in the way of command or reconnaissance machines was the justly famous half-ton Dodge command car. What was sought was something more agile and a good deal lighter. Word went out to industry together with a set of design parameters, the request to get cracking and a deadline set for late 1940. Out of approximately 135 vehicle and equipment manufacturers, only American Bantam met the deadline with a prototype, but Willys-Overland and Ford came up with their versions shortly thereafter.

The designer of the first Bantam was professional consultant Karl Probst who had taken the temporary title of Chief Engineer with the firm. It took Probst a mere five days to fit the Army's parameters into a design that Bantam could produce and the first prototype was rolling just six weeks later. Getting quick approval, another 70 pre-production vehicles were built and went along on the infamous 1940/41 Louisiana maneuvers under the command of no less a personage than then-Colonel Dwight D. Eisenhower.

The Willys prototype—called the Quad—was designed, also to the Army requirements, by a

group under the late Delmar G. Roos, vice president, engineering. Seventy of these were sent to Camp Holabird, Maryland in November of 1940. These were equipped with the Willys L-head four-cylinder engine that was the normal powerplant for the firm's automobiles and it was this engine that was to power every Jeep vehicle built until the 1950s.

Ford really hadn't wanted to enter the program since they had long ago dropped the Model A and B and were into heavier, bigger cars. However, under pressure from the military, which wanted Ford's production capacity, Ford came up with their prototype, the GP Pygmy, and delivered the first one to Camp Holabird in late November, 1940.

Now it was evaluation time. Each vehicle had features considered favorable and each also had shortcomings. None met the weight requirement—which had been 1,300 lbs., a ridiculous figure for the state of the art of the time. The limit was raised to a more realistic 2,160 lbs. Each company was then given an order for 1,500 examples of the improved version of their prototypes incorporating features newly required by the Army. Ford later received an order for a further 2,150 when most of their lot were lend-leased to Britain. These were powered by a modified tractor engine with 119 cubic inches and a rousing 45 bhp at 3,600 rpm.

Willys engineers went back to the shop and the drawing board in Toledo and proceeded to pare 300-odd lbs. off their Quad to meet the weight limit. During the evaluation period it was found that the pared-down Willys came closest to suiting the requirements and it had the cheapest and best engine of the three. This was the Willys MA and, with modifications including bits and features from the others, was chosen as the final model—the famous MB. The other manufacturers then geared to produce the standardized vehicle and the vehicle that was to be known as the "World War II Jeep" was born.

What happened next was, to say the least, very unusual and as mentioned, technically illegal. With the Willys MB accepted as the standard and the Ford GP rejected, Ford was asked by the Quartermaster-General to go into production with the Willys. The reasons, of course, were Ford's production capacity and assurance that the quarter-tonner would continue to roll off the line even if Willys-Overland was sabotaged. Edsel Ford gave the go-ahead and Ford went into production with what they

called the GPW—for general purpose Willys.

During the ensuing years the Willys MB was used for almost everything a wheeled machine in wartime could be used for. It was armed with a variety of guns and used as a fighting vehicle, it was used as an ambulance, as a scout car and as just plain transportation for anyone who could get his hands on one either officially or not. To be assigned a personal jeep was to be assigned a treasure beyond price and the methods taked to assure continuing possession would make a Corvette owner's precautions against theft seem like an open invitation by comparison. By the war's end there was hardly a man in service who hadn't at one time or another had a desire to have one of his very own. The fact that you can still find MBs and GPWs in use to this day attests to the validity of the desire. About the only force that can actually destroy one is rust.

As for the Willys MB's present-day name, "Jeep," its origin is even more obscure. The only thing—other that present ownership—that is sure is that it was originally a Popeye cartoon character, a popular creature who was neither flesh nor fowl, who had all the answers to any problem and who could do anything. We remember an assistant professor of military science who absolutely insisted in 1941 that the Dodge half-ton command car was a Jeep and the quarter-tonner was a Peep. Minneapolis-Moline Power Implement Co. had supplied a modified tractor in 1940 that active duty National Guardsmen at Camp Ripley, Minnesota, dubbed a Jeep; the companies even tried to advertise the claim, but they and the good soldier-teacher were running counter to the popular thought. By 1942 the name belonged firmly to the truck, half-ton, 4x4 and was given official cachet by appearing in a 1942 Training Manual.

In the meantime, Willys-Overland pulled off the commercial coup of the decade and perhaps the century simply by registering the name as a trademark of the Willys-Overland Corporation. After the war, so taken were its former users that Willys-Overland was able to put into production the first "universal Jeep," the CJ-2A and sell them as fast as they could bolt them together.

At one point they went a little too far in their institutional advertising when they claimed that their engineers, in conjunction with the Army, had "created and perfected the jubilant Jeep." As they hadn't given credit to other groups involved, a Federal Trade Commission

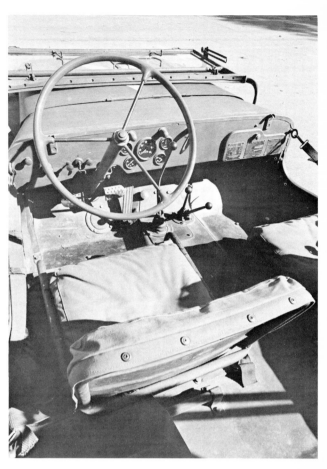

Instrument gauges were not internally lighted. Instead, illumination was provided by hooded exterior bulbs (which usually did not work).

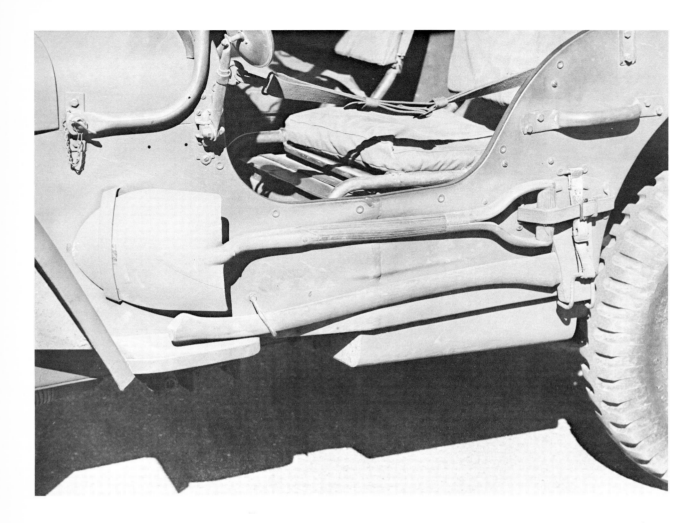

complaint was registered and, after five years of investigation, a cease and desist order was issued. They actually did come up with the standardized MB and they did indeed build more Jeeps than all the others put together but American Bantam actually built the first prototype. All Willys could fairly claim as their very own was the engine.

Be that as it may, the act of registering the trademark was a stroke of genius. How many other cars or trucks have had the most popular vehicle of their era as a promotion piece and demonstrator and a global war for their launching?

1909 Ford Model T

1909 FORD MODEL T

Engine Type: L-head in-line 4-cylinder
Displacement: 176.7 cubic inches (2.8 liters)
Horsepower: 20
Transmission: 2-speed manual
Wheelbase: 100 inches
Overall Length: 132 inches
Overall Height: 93 inches
Overall Width: 69 inches

If you are under forty, you probably have little idea of what Henry Ford's Model T did for America. If you are under thirty, the "T" may just be a freak—a black, tinny, spindly car that older neighbors used to haul out for Fourth of July parades and talk about after a few beers with a fondness that seemed, at best, unreasonable. Why?

Well, put the number fifteen million between your ears. Fifteen million is a lot of anything and Henry Ford built that many Model Ts between 1909 and 1927. The first person to bring up the Volkswagen's production figures as a comparison might as well forget it. Ford built those 15,000,000 Model Ts at a time when there was little serious mass production machinery, no huge milling machines that could spit out finished engine blocks like so many watermelon seeds. Face it, even if you are a Chevrolet fan, Henry Ford and his Model T put this country on wheels. Period.

The Model T wasn't Ford's first car, of course. Before the T got underway in 1909, there were several failures, one of which eventually grew into the Cadillac Motor Co. But when Ford slapped a $500 price tag on a four-cylinder Model N roadster at the New York Auto Show in 1905, he became part of history. That opened the door for Henry Ford, and his next act was the Model T.

In 1909, the automobile was having trouble existing as anything more than a rich man's toy. The average cost of a car was over $2100 and the common worker earned $10 to $15 a week. Ford, with his fast-developing mass production techniques, gave those workers a remarkably cheap, durable, steel-bodied automobile. America responded by flooding Mr. Ford with orders for his inexpensive car. It took quite a while to catch up, but the public didn't mind—they just wanted a Ford.

For fourteen years after 1909, Model Ts ruled the sales charts—and with good reason. Not only was the Model T durable and inexpensive, but also Ford managed gradually to lower Model T prices. The touring car started at $950 in 1909, slipped to $525 by 1918 and was down to $380 by 1926. It was that kind of thinking that gave Ford a favored edge for years.

By 1926, William Knudsen of Chevrolet had seen the automotive tastes of the working class outgrow the Model T. Ford's sales peaked in 1923 and had begun to sink. In the late twenties, a very famous battle over the future of the T developed between the senior Ford and his son Edsel. The heir to the Ford empire felt that the T was outdated and should be replaced. In the end, the senior Ford acquiesced. In 1927, Ford closed the factory for almost six months and reopened with the Model A.

It seems to us, half a century removed from the fact, that every Model T ever built looked the same. Actually, there were variations in body type ranging from open roadsters to "Tudor" and "Fordor" sedans. And the car changed from

1909 Model T Ford Touring Car
Owner: Harrah's Automobile Collection
Photographer: John Lamm

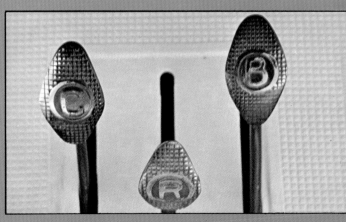

year to year as well. There were brass radiators and red paint in 1909, and it wasn't until 1914 that the customer was allowed "Any color you want as long as it's black." But things brightened up again in the twenties as Ford responded to the Chevrolet threat; in 1925, nickel-plated radiators and racy two-tone paint jobs were offered.

Red paint, nickel-plating, or basic black, the Model T always retained its most important feature—simplicity. The engine was a side-valve design with 176.7 cubic inches and about twenty horsepower. It had the esthetics of an anvil and was about as rugged, since most everything was cast iron and cheap. A replacement valve cost fifteen cents; a new block went for twenty dollars.

The two-speed planetary transmission (which was basically the same design as current automatics), was an innovation in 1909 (and a drawback in the twenties), but few of us would know how to drive it. Ford's system had three pedals, the high- and low-speed clutch pedal on the left, the reverse pedal in the middle and the foot brake on the right. To the left of the driver was a combination emergency brake and clutch-release lever.

The plan was to get the car running in neutral (a problem in itself), set the steering column-mounted hand throttle (in fact, the only throttle), and to push down on the clutch pedal to put the car in low gear. After you reached top speed in low, you let out the pedal and the transmission shifted to high (or "direct drive"). To stop, you slowed the car with the brake pedal, pulled back the emergency brake/clutch lever to get the car in neutral and, when everything had stopped, set the emergency brake.

The car's construction was simple. The 100-inch wheelbase frame had two parallel beams with a few crossmembers. There was a solid axle in back, an I-beam axle in front and transverse springs at both ends. The axles were located by two radius rods each. The pair in front ran back from the wheels to the center of the chassis. The pair in back did the reverse, running from the center of the chassis back to the wheels. It was called Ford's Three-Point Suspension and their ads likened it to a three-legged milking stool.

There was one point on which the old timers never spoke of the "T" kindly. As Bellamy Partridge wrote in *Fill 'er Up!*:

> Starting the motor was a problem. Tickle the carburetor, hold the choke wire at exactly the

right spot—a hairsbreadth either way would spoil the combination. Draw a long breath and hold it—this was supposed to protect you in case of backfire. Then give a sudden yank on the starting crank. This had to be done just so. It wasn't a pull or a push—it was rather a flip or a flirt. You had to take the engine by surprise—make a quick deliver—and then step back out of reach. Cranking was something that had to be learned by long practice, for it was a fine art like a sinker or a knuckle ball.

Getting sloppy meant a strained back, or occasionally a broken arm.

The rest was bouncing and creaking and flat tires. It all sounds a bit grim, what with only 1,000 miles on a set of tires, but it was the only way in the early decades of this century. There were only a few paved roads when the Model T first started, so the car was geared low to help it get out of ruts and quagmire roads. Someone once commented that the T was geared so low it was the fastest car on earth for the first three feet. But it worked, and in 1909, that's what mattered.

Most of the original roads and mechanical problems fell by the roadside, as they say, in the Model T's declining years. The same simple ruggedness that fashioned the T's success before World War I was overkill in the twenties.

The driver of a Model T will find spark and throttle handles on the steering column, the coil box on the dash, and the clutch release/emergency brake handle on the left. The three pedals on the floor are part of the transmission system.

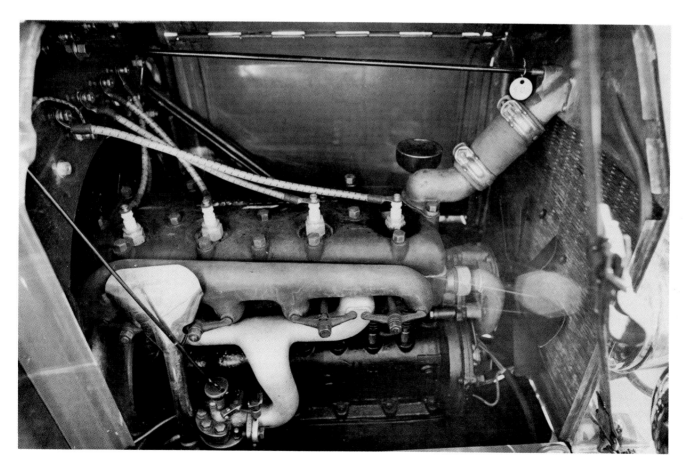

The Model T engine was, above all, simple; it was made mostly of cast iron and developed about 20 horsepower.

Some say it was the planetary transmission alone that killed the car. The bands in the transmission overheated easily and a long trip might find the owner changing them two or three times.

So by 1926, the Model T's time was up. It had served its purpose, putting us on the road much as the Renault 4CV and the Morris Minor would do for France and England, respectively, after World War II.

Sadly, hundreds of thousands of the Model Ts were junked in the thirties. The Model A and its competitors were trying so hard to outdo each other that the automobile progressed at a mind-boggling rate. The T became a disposable car and they were scrapped for five dollars apiece. One popular song moaned, "Poor Lizzie . . . What'll Become of You Now?"

The Model T today? There are perhaps a few less than 200,000 left, but they are priced considerably higher than five dollars now. In fact, one of our contributors just sold his mint-condition T to a European collector for $10,000. *Touché.*

1911 Renault A-X Roadster

1911 RENAULT A-X ROADSTER

Engine Type: L-head in-line 2-cylinder

Displacement: 1.1 liters (67 cubic inches)

Horsepower: 9

Transmission: 3-speed manual

Wheelbase: 95 inches

Overall Length: 132 inches

Overall Height: 58 inches

Overall Width: 54 inches

You can just barely hear the faint "chunka-chunka-chunka" coming through the cold air of Paris in 1898 as twenty-one-year-old Louis Renault guides his first *voiturette* (little automobile), the 3/4-horsepower engine huffing and clunking, up to the curb. Everyone wants a ride in the novel horseless carriage and Louis obliges. He sells the car to the first rider—before the night is over, he has orders for twelve more.

That little scene was played again countless times around the turn of the century, by hundreds of bicycle repairmen, engine builders, and general tinkerers who put together all sorts of horseless contraptions. But Louis and company were different. One reason was nestled under the driver/rider seat, an honest-to-God transmission, the first ever to link the steadily turning automobile engine with the sometimes stationary wheels . . . no more noisy and unreliable belts or chains. Louis shared his second distinction with a small number of other men—he continued to build automobiles. In fact, he thrived on it.

Five years later Louis Renault led the 1903 Paris-Madrid Race as he roared his lightweight racer to the checkpoint at Bordeaux. However, there he learned that his brother, Marcel, had been gravely injured. The team cars were withdrawn in honor of the Renault brother, who, deep in a coma, soon died. But it made little difference. That last of the major city-to-city races had already killed and maimed too many people and the French government stopped it at Bordeaux. The race cars were ordered shipped back to Paris by train.

Saddened, Louis, who had officially formed the firm as Renault Frères (the Renault Brothers) considered quitting the business, selling it all. But a third brother, Fernand, sold his business to devote full time to the automobile company.

The important point is that it all happened in 1903. Just five years after Louis had "chunka-chunked" down the Rue de Helder on that cold December night, he had started the company, run his lightweight race cars to the top finishing positions in many of the major races in Europe, pushed production to 1,000 cars per year and was ready to quit, leave an industry many people didn't even know really existed.

Only five of the present U.S. manufacturers can claim roots that extend back to 1903. Oldsmobile can point to a heritage that roughly parallels Louis Renault's. Thomas B. Jeffery had mustered enough financial support in 1902 to launch what would one day become American Motors. Henry Leland started Cadillac in 1903, the same year an ex-plumber, David Buick, got his automobile into production, while a racer named Henry Ford was putting together his motor company. There would be eight years of Renaults produced after Marcel's death before any Chevrolets were produced, and the rest of our manufacturers started after that. The Renault was a very early automobile.

In Retrospect

1911 Renault A-X Roadster   Owner: Hillcrest Motor Co.
Photographed for Motor Trend by John Lamm

It was also a very pretty automobile, especially for the period, when so many automobiles looked drab and uninteresting. We first saw the car about a year ago, when Eric Dahlquist and I stopped in at Hillcrest Cadillac in Beverly Hills to look over the antique cars they had on display in their showroom. Jimmy Duffy, who watched over the collection, showed us the Renault, commenting that in 1965 the Antique Automobile Club of America judged it the best restored foreign automobile in the U.S. We saw other cars from the collection as well—a Regal Underslung, a Ferrari Barchetta, a

stately Minerva, and a clutch of fascinating old popcorn wagons—all restored piece by piece by Duffy, Bill Gates, Veto Ketchin and Tanis Peralta.

But when we went back last April to pick a car to photograph, I went straight to the Renault. It stands out in a crowd.

I think its attraction is the roadster body with the shining British Racing Green paint, classic Renault coffin nose, brass radiator back against the firewall, and the raked windshield. There's a good reason for the green, since the body was built by Cann of London. Underneath, it is the

To watch the road, the driver of the 1911 Renault Roadster either had to peer through the steering wheel or through the few inches of windscreen that extended above the wheel. Visibility with the top up left much to be desired.

1911 version of the Model AX, first introduced in 1905. There is a simple ladder-type steel frame with both front and rear axles bolted to semi-elliptic springs. Drive, as with all Renaults, is through Louis' three-speed transmission, a short driveshaft, then the rear end. Roughly the same as a modern sedan.

The engine is a side-valve-type L-head of Renault design, 1.1 liters, 2 cylinders. Nine horsepower and very straightforward for its day. That would mean individually cast cylinders mated to a common crankcase, horrendously long connecting rods, and external pushrods working off a cam mounted high in the crankcase. Of some note to the mechanically minded, there is pressure lubrication to the main bearings and the crankshaft is drilled so centrifugal force will drive oil to the big end bearings. The original carburetor was an updraft one-barrel patented by Renault, but the Hillcrest car has a Zenith replacement, a common switch. Ignition involved a high tension magneto firing Renault sparking plugs. The clutch was a leather-covered aluminum unit in the flywheel of the engine, said to require "practically no adjustment." Steering was of the

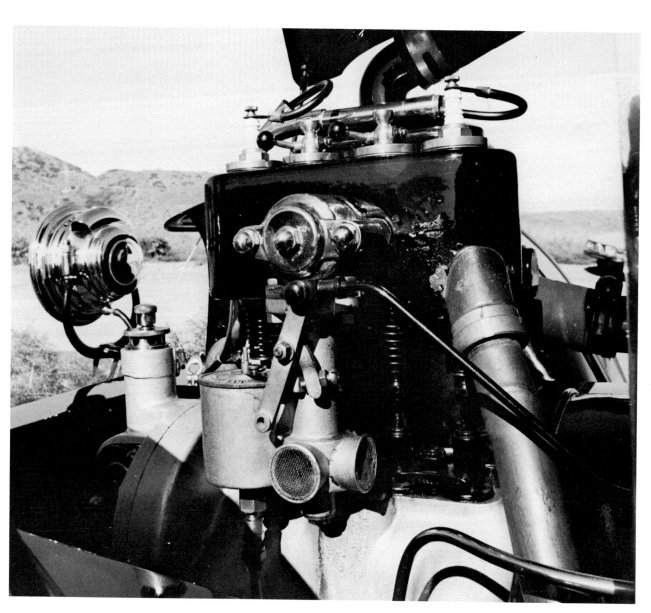

The Renault's nine-horsepower engine has two cylinders and pressure lubrication of the crankshaft.

screw and sector type, brakes were mechanical to the rear wheels only, and both worked on 7.10 x 90 Dunlop tires.

The Hillcrest car's interior is fitting for the era, with thick, tufted seats and a massive wooden steering wheel—a simple, plush environment, the wood of the wheel and cockpit adding a touch of warmth to the surroundings. There is only one functional door, the left one, the other being blocked by the spare tire. The seating position is upright, but, unlike other antique cars, you don't feel as though you are a good ten feet off the ground. The driver has to watch the road either through the steering wheel or in the very few inches between it and the windscreen. Visibility with top up is, at best, limited.

The Renault Company chunka-chunkaed through the years until 1944. De Gaulle is the man for France and Louis Renault is the man for prison, accused by the government of collaboration with the Germans. At sixty-seven, though, you can't expect (and others can't expect you) to last too long, and so within the year after he is locked up, Louis Renault, the Henry Ford of France, is dead. Perhaps this isn't the time to comment on postwar witchhunts or the proper definition of collaboration, but now some speculate perhaps the charges weren't all true and De Gaulle just had his heart set on nationalizing the company, which he did. But that is a discussion for another day.

1929 Ford Cabriolet

1929 FORD CABRIOLET

Engine Type: overhead valve in-line 4-cylinder
Displacement: 200.5 cubic inches (3.2 liters)
Horsepower: 80
Transmission: 3-speed manual
Wheelbase: 103.5 inches
Overall Length: 159 inches
Overall Height: 69 inches
Overall Width: 72 inches

Between the great wars there was more than the Florida land bubble, Lindbergh's flight, bread lines, a handful of Duesenbergs and all that jazz. There was also a car called the Model A Ford, for which you could buy as much after-market stuff as any small-block Chevy, and then some.

Americans have always preferred simple, clearcut answers to their problems. The Model A Ford met all these requirements. After nineteen years with the Model T, the whole U.S. population waited for the A with the kind of uneasy anticipation that today greets a new Volks-wagen Beetle—a promise too long postponed.

Yet, while VW still fumbles with one Beetle replacement prototype after another, the Model A Ford, an interim car before the V8, was more successful than its predecessor. The Lizzie assembly lines rolled out an astronomical 15 million in nearly two decades; the A did 4.5 million in just four years. Sprung on a 103 1/2-inch wheelbase, the machine retained the four-wheels-and-a-board-make-a-Ford posture of the T, but somehow managed to embody the timeless classic design strokes that marked

Dearborn's products until the late '40s. Just as the Beetle would, decades later, the A used an undersquare engine. With 3 7/8-inch x 4 1/4-inch bore-stroke, the 2,000.5 cu. in. four had one major overriding engineering advantage on its competitors: it always ran. With 4.0:1 compression and 40 horsepower at 2,200 lackadaisical rpm, the thing wore out slowly, very slowly. The whole, low-key approach legislated for a long stress-free life. Even if something did let go, anyone with basic, native Yankee mechanical ability could get the thing going again in an afternoon with simple hand tools.

And yet, with all these good things, there were people who wanted more, as people are wont to do. For openers, two outfits in Detroit, Briggs and Murray, built the special bodies for the Cabriolet and Town Car models Ford offered. Far from your any-color-as-long-as-it's-black jobs, these models incorporated the same sort of pizzaz as a Maverick Grabber with air. And then, if you were really a peer-group leader, you knocked 4 1/2 inches off the car's height by exchanging the 21-inch wheels for a set of 18-inch Chrysler wires and shaving the Cabriolet's rear top-bow down an inch-and-a-half.

You have to remember that Henry Ford was always a racer, and his cars, even the Model T, always possessed certain unique performance characteristics. Unburdened by complications like sound deadening, Fords were light and fitted with 3.78:1 rear axle ratios, would usually walk mammoths like Duesenbergs or Caddies—up to about 30 mph, where the big boys gathered steam and vacuumed off your doors.

In 1928, Harry Miller, the genius architect of the period, contributed to whooping up the Model A when he embarked on a five million dollar enterprise called Miller-Schofield, aimed at producing ultra-efficient aircraft engines and

In Retrospect

1929 Ford Cabriolet   Owner: Harrah's Automobile Collection
Photographed for Motor Trend by John Lamm

the nationwide distribution of Miller carburetors, aluminum pistons, and OHV cylinder heads for the brand-new Model A Ford. Part and parcel of the Miller-Schofield deal was Miller's brilliant designer Leo Goossen.

The most obvious barrier to whooping up the Model A engines was the L-block design's poor air-flow characteristics, a situation Goossen rectified with the Miller Hi-Speed head, a bolt-on, pushrod-operated overhead-valve head. An ingenious facet of the deal, besides the $137.50 price, was that Goossen incorporated readily available Buick rocker arms. With a single, 1 1/4-inch carburetor, hop-up ads of the period claimed a horsepower leap from 40 to 68 at 2,400 rpm.

The engine doesn't sound like a Model "A," even at idle; it's more like a junior version of Phil Hill's Blower Bentley with the ticking of the lash in the valves at low speed. Even if you hadn't looked under the hood, and even if the engine wasn't running, if you knew anything about "As," you'd know something was up. There is an Apco oil-pressure gauge, quite unnecessary on an oil-splash lubricated system. Besides the oil pressure monitor, the complement of instruments in the driver's kit is a speedometer, odometer, trip indicator, ammeter, gas gauge, and cigar lighter.

You sit high in the Model A, bolt upright—with a commanding view of the road beyond the gracefully sweeping fenders. Steering is light and quick with a fair amount of road shock, and when you get into the full lock, effort increases noticeably. Ford's traditional, transverse, semi-elliptic spring arrangement was never known to produce boulevard ride, but then the car isn't sloppy cornering either, sticking far beyond what you'd expect from five-inch tires with minuscule footprints.

Somehow it doesn't make any difference how old a car is. Once you find out its engine has been tricked up, you must try its mettle against some known value. Harrah's people ran the Miller-Schofield to 80 mph, but the real gut test is putting it on kids in Datsun and Toyota sedans at traffic lights. With bags of low-speed torque you leap away from the rest with a great rush of noise and flutter, and people wonder what kind of late-model engine has been grafted in. It was always easy to overdrive Ford mechanical brakes, and in this machine the danger is squared, at the very least.

Out on the highway the ride is generally a lot

Horsepower on a "whooped-up" Model A engine went from 40 to 68. Leo Goossen, a brilliant designer, was responsible for many of the changes that helped the engine produce the additional power.

smoother than you thought it would be and you find yourself wondering what it would have been like to have one in the early fall of 1929 when all the smart money had pulled out of Wall Street and Joseph P. Kennedy thoughtfully remarked that "only a fool holds out for the top dollar." You get to wondering, too, about basic automotive truths and where Detroit went sour—when cars began to be no fun to drive anymore.

1954 Corvette

1954 CORVETTE

Engine Type: overhead valve in-line 6-cylinder

Displacement: 235.5 cubic inches (3.8 liters)

Horsepower: 150

Transmission: 2-speed automatic

Wheelbase: 102 inches

Overall Length: 167 inches

Overall Height: 52 inches (top up)

Overall Width: 72 inches

Remember when Arthur Godfrey was about the only thing you could get on the radio? Remember when a dizzy, luscious blonde named Marilyn Monroe was starring in *Gentlemen Prefer Blondes*? Remember when Alan Ladd ordered strawberry sodapop in *Shane*? Or when the New York Yankees won the pennant for the fifth year in a row? You are remembering 1953.

Nineteen fifty-three was also a big year for auto racing. Bill Vukovich drove Howard Keck's Fuel Injection Special to first place in the Indianapolis 500 and some dude nicknamed "Gentleman Jim" Kimberley was trouncing all lesser sports car pilots with his expensive ex-works Ferraris.

Foreign cars with names nobody knew how to pronounce were capturing the imagination of American car "buffs." Sure, Bill Stroppe's Lincoln had finished first through fourth in the stock car class in the Pan-American road races in Mexico, but the real winners were the Germans in the gull-winged Mercedes 300SLs. And, over the barren Bonneville Salt Flats, a madcap Britisher named Donald Healey was setting all kinds of world records with a little four-cylinder Austin streamliner.

Such was the unlikely setting for the birth of America's one and only sports car, the Corvette—a car born of an incredible optimism, as touching as it was naive. Harley Earle, General Motors' first chief of styling, was the man behind the project. Recalling the hot rods of the dry lakes racers before the war, Earle had urged GM to create a car that would appeal not only to the hot rodders but to the newly emerging sports car enthusiast, those twits in tweeds driving spindly-wheeled MG TCs.

Earle put a small group of men to work on the project in 1951 and, although many contributed, Earle's influence dominated the final result, as evidenced by such touches as the "wraparound" windshield, first used by Earle on his LeSabre, the first GM "dream car." After gaining the approval of Harlow H. Curtice, then GM president, and Ed Cole, then Chevy's chief engineer (and now GM's president), a fiberglass show car was dummied up and shipped to New York for GM's road-show-style "motorama" display at the Waldorf-Astoria hotel.

The "dream car" was the hit of the show, especially with Ford engineers, who rushed back to Dearborn to whip up their own two-seater. Chevrolet decided that they had a winner and began work on a limited-production schedule, which would have the car in the showrooms by 1953.

In wanting to make the production car as much like the show car prototype as possible, Chevrolet was taking a risk. No manufacturer had ever made thousands of cars with fiberglass bodies. Chevrolet would abandon manufacture of the bodies after the first 300, turning the task over to an Ashtabula, Ohio, boat firm that still has the job today.

Why did Chevrolet opt for a plastic body?

Exhaust extensions were added to stock pipes so that the exhaust wouldn't blacken the rear of the car.

Cost, mostly. Tooling up for a steel body would have cost millions, while plastic body dies could be made for less than $400,000. Ironically, now that Corvette's annual production is 120 times the 1953 figure, Chevrolet may have decided that fiberglass bodies are no longer the most economical, even for a limited-production model; the '76 is rumored to be clothed in steel.

Because the fiberglass body was unstressed—adding nothing to the strength of the car—Chevy engineers had to determine a way to strengthen the standard sedan chassis the sports car was based on. Their solution was to lay two iron beams across the middle in a big "X" shape.

The low height of the car—less than three feet from the ground to the windowsill—created another challenge: how to fit in a radiator. Chevy ended up tilting a Chevy sedan radiator and designing a new barrel-shaped expansion tank to squeeze alongside the engine.

You would expect an all-new car to get an all-new engine, right? Wrong. Chevy's brass felt that the idea of a sports car with a plastic body was as far out as they wanted to go on that particular limb. So they reached into the parts bin and pulled out the venerable Stovebolt Six.

Of course, they gave it a sexy name—"The Blue Flame"—and treated it to a few hotrod type modifications. Juiced up with a high-lift cam, a giddy 8-to-1 compression ratio, dual exhausts, and three Carter side-draft carburetors, the good ol' Blue Flame Six put out 150 horses at 4,200 rpm.

Another bet hedged on the first Corvette was in the choice of the gearbox. Afraid a stick shift would limit the Corvette's appeal to too small a market, Chevy originally offered the Corvette with an automatic transmission only.

And, just to make sure you didn't mistake it for one of those rough-and-ready European sports cars, Chevy decked out each and every Corvette with white-wall tires and simulated knock-off wheel discs. For the first year, the only color you could get was polo white with a red leather interior. Later, Chevy relented and offered other color combinations.

The unique body style had a few surprises for the uninitiated. Like when you went to roll up a window and found out there were no windows. The Corvette, you see, was inspired by those foreign jobs with their plastic side curtains and . . . . But, you forgave them when you found the convertible top could be tucked neatly under a

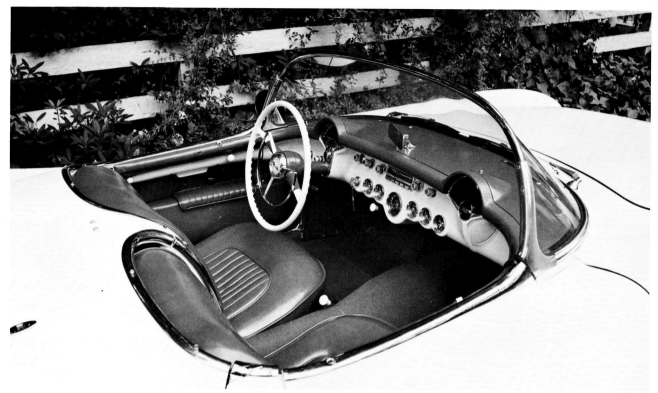

Although Chevrolet made an effort to include sophisticated instrumentation, the gauges are so small that they are nearly impossible to read unless the car is standing still.

fiberglass tonneau that left the back deck slick as a duck's tail.

In spite of the Flash Gordonized styling, which is appealing even today, a short jaunt in an early Corvette convinces you that Chevrolet was guilty of promising much more than the car could deliver. The controls were awkward. The steering wheel is the size of an old 78-rpm record and takes three-and-a-half muscle-straining turns to go lock-to-lock. The transmission is a two-speed automatic, Chevy's infamous PowerGlide. Mastering its vagaries is simple but taxing: Put your toes through the floorboard to keep it in low. When you reach the neighborhood of 55 mph, it will make a great leap forward into drive.

Instrumentation is a bad joke. Chevrolet made a valiant effort to include a tachometer and water temperature and oil pressure gauges, but all the dials are necker knob-sized and undecipherable unless the car is standing still —and even then you have to squint.

As for handling, although 3,200 lbs. is not unsupportable weight, the sedan-derived suspension—independent with coils up front and a solid axle with leaf springs in back—was designed for a cushy ride, not for tearing around

corners. Any attempt at haste produces gross understeer and strains the skinny 6.70 x 15 tires to their maximum.

Looking back, it's obvious that Chevrolet's Great White Hope was a technical antique, as compared to, say, the Jaguar XK-120, introduced way back in '49 or the '52 Mercedes-Benz 300SLs. But if Chevrolet was embarrassed at their buckeye naivete, they didn't let on. Instead, they offered a V-8 in '55, a 3-speed manual gearbox in '56, fuel injection in '57 and . . . well, you know the rest.

The mint '54 shown here belongs to Lee Nicholl, who at nineteen is too young to remember the fifties. But when Lee was ten, his older brother bought a '54 Corvette and Lee caught the fever. Inheriting this car as a "hand-me-down" two years later, Lee began a painstaking restoration of the car in the hope that it would be done by the time he received his driver's license—a teenager's passport to paradise.

But in restoration, success depends on what you started with. When Lee found a better '54, he bought it. After two years' work, it is as you see it now.

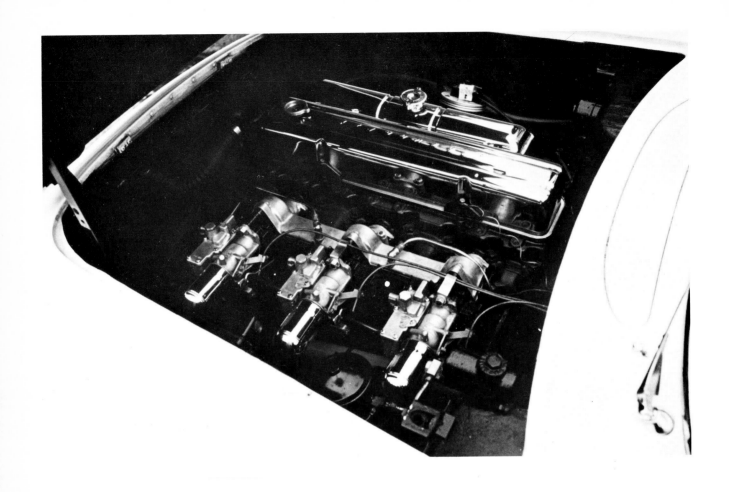

1929 Type 37A Bugatti

1929 TYPE 37A BUGATTI

Engine Type: single overhead cam in-line 4-cylinder, supercharged

Displacement: 1.5 liters (91.5 cubic inches)

Horsepower: 90 (estimated)

Transmission: 4-speed manual

Wheelbase: 94.3 inches

Overall Length: 150 inches

Overall Height: 46 inches

Overall Width: 68 inches

You may have an inkling as to how fast or successful the Bugatti was, but have you ever thought how beautiful? Bathed by that solitary light in the Hillcrest Cadillac garage is perhaps the most beautiful Grand Prix racing machine ever built. Drink in the simple, unfiltered beauty of the cast aluminum wheels, as much a Bugatti trademark as their horseshoe-shaped radiator. Notice the leather strap holding the sidemount wheel; the delicate stainless steel safety wire lacing along the bottom, bordered by more louvers than any street rod in the world. No wonder, then, men have actually parked Bugattis in their living rooms just for sheer visual appreciation.

Under the hood there is the sculptured, squared-off, aluminum engine all polished and set in an engine-turned compartment. It is a monster to live with and work on, but the Bugatti owners could care less. Even the car's detractors, fans of Delage, Sunbeam, and Mercedes-Benz Grand Prix cars, who complain that the Bugatti won so many races because they had enough cars in enough races at the right time, usually won't argue with the esthetics.

This body shape lasted virtually unchanged from 1924 to 1932, spanning all the variations of the Type 35, Type 37, Type 39 and Type 51 models. Only a serious Bugattiste can point out the external differences between the eight-cylinder Types 35, 39, and 51 and the four-cylinder Type 37 and their supercharged offshoots, but only an expert cares.

Ironically, in point of actual fact, the exquisite and successful Bugattis did not always reflect the zenith of contemporary engineering. The British publication *Autocar*, in the introduction to an article by the Bugatti expert, Hugh G. Conway, quipped:

> W.O. Bentley might well have described the Bugatti as the triumph of artistry over engineering principles. Bugatti's standard of finish is a delight to the eye and to the touch. Although sometimes appearing to deviate from accepted good engineering practice the better to achieve visual effect, Bugatti cars have always been remarkably effective and a great pleasure to their owners.

Conway himself wrote,

> Indeed there is a natural temptation to wonder how designs so poor from some points of view could have been so successful. The answer as in most things is that sheer performance is not everything; reliability and availability are often as important. He seems to be agreeing with some of the critics, but then the race ends when the flag drops and now, 40 years later, all that really matters are the records and the totals, like an unimaginable 1049 Bugatti victories in 1926 and 1927.

Three of the best of the string of models—types 35, 37, and 39—look identical. The Type 35 was the first, though even in 1922 its engine was a bit antiquated, Bugatti spurning the twin-cam, inclined-valve Ballot layout (still used in modern Offy and Foyt engines) in favor of a single overhead cam working each cylinder's two intake and single exhaust valves through

1929 Type 37A Bugatti
Owned by Hillcrest Cadillac   Photographed for *Motor Trend,* by John Lamm

rocker levers. The engine was cast in two blocks of four and the crankshaft spun in large ball bearings. The first engines had plain babbited bearings for the big ends of the connecting rods, but they were replaced by incredibly expensive roller bearings. There were two engine sizes (121.3. cu. in. and 140 cu. in.) but several horsepower levels ranging from a mere 70 hp to a supercharged 130 hp.

Bugatti wanted to replace the older Brescia model sports car for 1926 with one that looked like the Grand Prix Type 35, so he built a 91-cubic inch, four-cylinder version and dubbed it the Type 37. A year later he added a supercharger and our centerspread car, the Type 37A, was off racing. Standard Bugatti valve layout was carried over from the Type 35's Eight, but the high-priced roller bearings were passed up in favor of plain versions. From a model that did not start out to be a racer, the 37A moved into the record books as one of the more successful Bugatti racing cars. One brave soul even set one up to lap the high banks of Brooklands at 122 mph. That had to have been a bit terrifying, looking out over the field of louvers past those skinny 27-inch Dunlop tires with all that negative camber, knowing that if something went wrong . . . the horrors of hindsight. Perhaps it was the exhilaration of listening to that little Roots' charger ram the mixture of gas and benzol through the screaming four that made it worth it. Perhaps we shouldn't ask.

The car's next reincarnation was as the Type 51 and there is a good portion of American thought in this engine. Ettore Bugatti's son, Jean, had grown to be as good an engineer as his father was an artist. Jean convinced his father that if Bugatti wanted to keep up, the old man would have to abandon the single overhead cam arrangement. It was 1929 and American "Leon Duray" (actually a cover name for George Stewart) was traveling in Europe with two front-wheel-drive Miller race cars. Called the Packard Cable Specials, the Millers ran impressively at Monza, Italy, before breaking, and after the race Bugatti offered Duray a trade. The financially overextended American got three Type 43 sports cars (which looked like a four-seat version of the Type 35) and passage home in exchange for the two Millers. Bugatti adapted freely from the twin-cam, 2-valve-per-cylinder Miller head/cylinder-block combination, grafting it to roughly the same blower, crankcase, and crankshaft as the old Eight. Horsepower in the

new 140-cubic-inch engine shot to 170 and the forty or so Type 51s constructed were the most successful racing cars Bugatti built, staying at the front of the starting grid until the German domination of Grand Prix racing in 1934-35.

To last that long on the ulcer-breeding Grand Prix circuits, the basic race car that became the Types 35, 37, 39, and 51 had to be special mechanically, but that wasn't necessarily the case. Despite its looks, the car had several outmoded features or pieces that became a bit old-fashioned over the car's eight-year model run. Bugatti was never one to spurn a proven thing. His original reversed quarter-elliptic spring rear suspension was dynamite when new, but almost a liability at the end. He refused to adapt hydraulic brakes to his cars, so it took strong legs on cable-operated brakes to haul the cars down. In fact, Bugatti designed his famous aluminum alloy wheels with brake drums attached so that when a car pitted for new tires it also got new brakes. Several of his engines had non-removable heads.

Perhaps the cars succeeded because they were small, light, and simple. The wheelbase is only 94.3 inches, the front track 47.1 inches, and weight, depending on engine and equipment, in the area of 1,650 pounds. But they were (and are) magnificent cars and they have an air of purity about them. In this racing period of airfoils, wings, and extra aerodynamic devices, it is interesting to look back at such a pure design. Granted, Bugatti didn't have to contend with today's speeds, but one has the feeling he would have fought having to use those "unnatural" devices. "Le Patron," as Bugatti's workers

With a supercharger, the type 37A aluminum engine once got a 37A Bugatti up to 122 mph on a banked track.

called him, even hated to use a supercharger on his cars, arguing they were morally wrong because they forced air into the engine, illegally increasing engine size. Morality? In a race car?

It is an interesting avenue of approach, but the kind of thing you have to expect when you have an artist designing a race car. That and perhaps the most beautiful racing cars ever built.

Corvette Sting Ray

CORVETTE STING RAY

Engine Type: overhead valve V-8

Displacement: 377 cubic inches (6.1 liters)

Horsepower: 550

Transmission: 4-speed manual

Wheelbase: 92 inches

Overall Length: 175.3 inches

Overall Height: 31.5 inches

Overall Width: 68.6 inches

In 1958 William L. Mitchell, head of GM's styling staff, acquired the famous chassis of the Corvette SS Mule that had seen so many pre-race laps in 1957 and had, in its moment in the sun, been test-hopped by Juan Fangio and Stirling Moss. That was the beginning of the Corvette Sting Ray.

Mitchell's beginning had been many years earlier. In 1934, he had come to New York City by way of Carnegie Tech and the Art Students League. He came from Pennsylvania, where his father sold Buicks. The young William L. Mitchell was also interested in automobiles, and spent hours outside the Park Avenue showrooms of the great automotive marques—admiring, absorbing, and later sketching the elegant custom-bodied cars of the day.

Mitchell pinned some of his automotive drawings on the wall of his cubicle at the Barron Collier Company. They drew the attention of the sons of the senior Collier, who by chance were among the greatest enthusiasts in America for road racing in the European style. Caught up in the Colliers' enthusiasm, Bill Mitchell made sketches of their racing events at the "Ring"

with MGs, Amilcars, and Willys and Ford specials, lively and spontaneous drawings that greatly pleased the youthful racers.

When Harley Earle, on the lookout for talent to expand his Art and Color Section at General Motors, saw some of Bill's drawings, a career was born. Mitchell was hired by GM as a sytlist, and soon showed himself one of the most energetic and able men in this new profession. When Earle retired on December 1, 1958, Mitchell, then forty-six, was named his successor as the head of GM's Styling staff.

Although Mitchell has never been in a position to race himself, he never lost his deep-seated enthusiasm for racing cars and the men who drive them. He had been a motivating force, starting in 1956, in the creation of modified Corvettes like the SR-2, which saw a lot of competition action through 1958, handled by Jim Jeffords, among others.

As sometimes happens, Mitchell and GM Styling were able to obtain, in 1958, an experimental Chevrolet chassis that was no longer required for its original purpose. It was a famous chassis, that of the Corvette SS Mule, which had been test-driven by Juan Manuel Fangio and Stirling Moss. After Sebring, the Mule chassis was completely cleaned up and refurbished, in a first stage of preparation for a planned assault on Le Mans. So, when the cancellation of all Chevrolet racing plans made the erstwhile Mule SS chassis free, Bill Mitchell acquired it and rebodied and redesigned it for racing privately.

The car had to be rebodied so it couldn't be immediately recognized. Under Bill's supervision, the main motif for the revived SS was adapted by stylist Larry Shinoda from the imaginative new design created in the Research Studio in 1957 for the stillborn Q-Corvette. It had the same low, wide grille and sharp-edged

RETROSPECT

1959 Corvette Sting Ray
Owned by General Motors Corporation
Photographed for *Motor Trend* by John Lamm

cross section with prominent bulges for clearance above the wheels.

During the winter of 1958–59 a fiberglass body was hand-laid for the car in the GM Styling fabrication shop. Given bonded-in reinforcements of annealed aluminum, the skin was conservatively heavy at 0.125-inch thick, about the same as a stock Corvette. Ducts at the sides of the wide front grille were arranged to feed fresh air to the fuel injection and also to the front brakes, and flush inlets in the rear deck admitted air to ducts that cooled the inboard rear brakes.

For engine cooling a prototype of the new Harrison aluminum radiator for the standard Corvette was used, angled sharply forward. Of the warm air departing from it, about one-third was deflected up through outlets atop the hood, while the rest flowed back through the engine room and the vents for the exhaust pipes to flush out the heat that had been so debilitating to the driver at Sebring. The exhaust headers were grouped more closely together so they were less effective as radiators, and were given additional shielding. As a final heat barrier, the firewall was carefully sealed and covered with a half-inch layer of Microquartz insulation, held in place by wire mesh.

The rebodied SS was aptly named the Sting Ray. It became Mitchell's personal property and he personally financed its racing activities. For this reason, as well as the fact that high-performance engine development at Chevrolet had been momentarily braked, the Sting Ray raced with an engine much like that used by the SS in 1957. Still 283 cubic inches in size, it was rated at 280 net horsepower at the clutch, installed, at 6,200 rpm. Peak torque was at 4,400 rpm, and the normal shift point was 6,500 revolutions per minute with 6,800 permissible in top gear. Experimental aluminum heads of several different types were used successfully on the Sting Ray engines, with an 11.0 to 1 compression ratio.

In all its drive line and chassis details, the Sting Ray was essentially identical to the SS. In the cockpit this was betrayed only by the deep-dished three-spoke steering wheel. Otherwise the panel was very simple (unlike that of the highly styled SS). While the car was raced it carried a Sting Ray emblem and name plate, but nowhere was there an obvious reference to Corvette or Chevrolet. The car was not a stalking horse for a covert GM return to racing;

in fact, Mitchell had to put on record, for GM management, a passionate yet plausible written argument in favor of his being allowed to enter the car on a personal basis before they would permit him to proceed.

Mitchell entered his glossy-red Sting Ray for the President's Cup Race at Maryland's twisty little Marlboro Raceway on April 18, 1959. Dr. Dick Thompson was the nominated driver, and Zora Arkus-Duntov was also in reluctant attendance—reluctant because he knew the chassis he had helped create would be competing in a kind of racing for which it had not been designed and without the level of factory support it was intended to have.

The Sting Ray ran four other events during 1959, driven by Thompson, with two interesting exceptions: John Fitch, the only American to drive on the Mercedes-Benz Grand Prix team, filled in for one race, while Anatole Lapine, now chief stylist at Porsche, teamed with Thompson for a 500-miler at Elkhart Lake.

All suffered the same Sting Ray problems: brakes and excessive weight. The first was problem enough, but the second compounded it. The brakes were drums and despite sintered metallic linings, which were eventually welded to the shoes, the problem lasted throughout the car's racing career. At the end of the 1959 season, 75 pounds were removed from the Sting Ray by a new 0.060-inch thick fiberglass body. With braking system changes, this reduced the car's dry weight to 2,000 pounds.

For the 1960 campaign, run from a rented shop in the back of a woodworking company in Roseville, Michigan, the chief mechanic was R. Ken Eschebach. Ken, Mitchell, Thompson, and Dean Bedford planned a major attack on the SCCA's National Championship in the C-Modified class, for cars with engines of from three to five liters. They were highly successful, taking their class and staging classic battles between Thompson and Augie Pabst in a B-Modified Scarab.

In 1961, the racer reverted to a show car. The Styling Staff spruced it up with a flush-fitting tonneau cover and a wrap-around canopy for the driver's side. It was given "Corvette" and "Fuel Injection" emblems and painted and polished to a fare-thee-well for its official debut on the show circuit at Chicago's McCormick Place in February, 1961. This marked the return to the Chevrolet fold of their prodigal motorcar. When it ceased being a novel show attraction it

Dr. Dick Thompson drives the original Sting Ray at the 1960 Riverside Grand Prix. The car's most famous battles, however, were in the Midwest.

was equipped with a passenger-side windscreen, a speedometer, and a rear license-plate mount, and Mitchell drove it to and from work when the weather was fair.

The veteran chassis was given several technical transplants during the sixties. Dunlop disc brakes were somehow fitted in. It was powered by a larger-displacement small-block engine, then by a Mark IV 427-cubic-inch V-8 with quadruple Weber carburetors under a transparent plastic air scoop. It was bright red again, for a while, until Mitchell decided he wanted to return it to the silver, smooth-hooded shape that had thrilled so many racing fans during its two years of open competition—years that Mitchell had unashamedly enjoyed.

1931 Cord L-29

1931 CORD L-29

Engine Type: L-head in-line 8-cylinder

Displacement: 298.6 cubic inches (4.8 liters)

Horsepower: 115

Transmission: 3-speed manual

Wheelbase: 137.75 inches

Overall Length: 197 inches

Overall Height: 61.5 inches

Overall Width: 72 inches

The owner's manual for the 1929 front-wheel-drive Cord L-29 began: "This car is not an experiment."

The line provides an interesting perspective. You have to remember that around the turn of the century, in the automobile's first years, many different layouts and drivelines were experimented with, inventors trying to figure out the best way to transform the buggy into the automobile. Yet by 1929, convention so dictated a front engine and rear-wheel drive that the front-drive Cord was an automobile apart. Not that Errett Lobban Cord and his engineers felt they had created an oddball. According to them, it was the other automobiles that were doing it wrong. In drawing the burden instead of pushing it, the Cord simply reverts to the natural method of moving a wheeled conveyance.

Whether oddball or revolutionary, the front-drive L-29 was the car you'd expect to bear the name Cord. When the L-29 was introduced in 1929, Cord was only thirty-four years old, and he'd been in and out of the automobile business since his teens. With $20 in his pocket at the age

of twenty-four, he began selling Moon automobiles in Chicago. Within five years, they were saying that Cord was the most successful automobile salesman in the country. His yearly commissions ran as high as $30,000, a fortune in those days. But he saw the string running out at Moon (which eventually died while struggling with the other front-drive car of the era, the Ruxton) and thought there might be more to the production side of the industry. That and his reputation brought him in touch with Chicago investor Ralph Bard, who just happened to have a dying automobile manufacturer on his books. It didn't look promising, but Cord took control of the Auburn Automobile Company.

He cleaned out Auburn's ugly 1924 models and replaced them with more expensive, $2,300 models that were as quick as they were fancy. The cars sold, profits climbed, Cord cornered a good majority of Auburn stock, and the fun began. It's important at this point to remember the time frame—the late twenties. The stock market was still spiraling upward and it was common for empires to be built and embellished just by trading stock. So using very little cash, Cord was able to expand his holdings, trading Auburn stock for controlling interests in numerous smaller companies. Along the way he added, among others, the Duesenberg Motor Co., Lycoming Mfg. Co., Limosine Body Co., even the Stinson Aircraft Co. In the last months of 1928, that gave Cord, through Auburn, assets over a very cool $11 million.

The L-29 was the third car in Cord's growing manufacturing empire, supplementing the Auburn and the Duesenberg, and some say its development was overseen by Cord himself. From the start he wanted a car in the Cadillac class, but one with something distinctive. Front-wheel drive came across as the best answer,

RETROSPECT

1931 Cord L-29
Owned by Ralph Evans
Photographed for *Motor Trend* by John Lamm

offering not only innovation but also a body low enough to undercut the size of the massive Packards, Cadillacs, and Lincolns.

The front-drive unit was the heart of the L-29. To get it, Cord went to one of the few men in the country who had done any serious research on the subject, Harry Miller. The Indianapolis 500 was Miller's test bed, and various cars of Miller design took all but one of the first ten places in the 1926 race. The Cord front-drive was developed around Miller's patents leading with the differential and with a conventional Detroit Gear & Machine three-speed transmission mounted on its side between the final drive and the Lycoming straight-eight engine.

It was the huge powerplant that dictated the L-29's long, drawn-out hood. The differential/transmission/engine was so long that a recess had to be cut in the firewall to accommodate it. A short crankshaft engine such as a V-8 might have been used to keep the whole driveline package more compact, but Cord preferred to stick with the stock Lycoming hardware (remember, he owned that company, too). The engine for the L-29 was the FD model, a 298.6-cubic-inch L-head that managed 115 horsepower at 3,300 rpm. It was a solid, adequate engine, equivalent in stature to General Motors' present-day 455-cubic-inch powerplant, which, in several forms, powers the larger GM models. Somehow, though, in a car such as the L-29 you would expect more, particularly considering the twin-cam straight six that powered its stablemate, the Duesenberg.

While front-drive was a bold selling point in the Cord's catalog, it was not totally successful. Although race cars can be built to satisfy a pure engineering idea, passenger cars have to be built with allowances for both ride and handling. This resulted in a difficult paradox for the front-drive designer in the days before independent suspension. Hence, the L-29 had a large solid front axle that was bowed forward to clear the bulging front-drive unit. Cord's engineers mounted the front brakes inboard to lower unsprung weight, a factor that bore directly on greater ride comfort. While it may have smoothed the ride, it put tremendous loads on the driveshaft's universal joints, furthering maintenance problems. And if there was one complaint about the L-29, it was keeping that front-drive in order.

There was another problem with the Cord and its pull-rather-than-push attitude—steep inclines. Since the car's long driveline spread its weight so far back on the frame, the L-29 had almost half its weight on the front wheels. When you started uphill and the weight bias shifted even more rearward, traction suffered. Try a steep hill covered with wet, slippery leaves and you might find yourself turning around and backing up.

Aside from that occasional hassle, they say the L-29 was delightful to drive once you learned how. The steering required considerable muscle and you had to be careful about getting on or off the throttle in a high-speed corner. Once the technique was mastered, though, the L-29 would corner with any luxury sedan in America.

Aside from the front-drive, which suffered from the state-of-the-engineering-art and materials in 1929, the L-29 matched the mechanical standards of its luxury class. A solid channel frame formed the car's base and the quality of the mechanical pieces, such as the I-beam rear axle and Lockheed hydraulic four-wheel brakes were fitting for its type. More important to the buyers, though, were the bodies that Cord added to that frame. As with the Ruxton, so with the Cord: because of the elimination of the conventional driveshaft and rear differential, the car could be built lower, closer to the ground than anything around in 1929, a good ten inches lower than the average Cadillac sedan of the time. And that long driveline, for all the havoc it played on weight distribution, was perfect for a body designer in the era of the long hood—the L-29's hood stretched almost six feet from grille to windshield. The tall, eighteen-inch wire wheels, with their knock-off hubs, made the body seem even lower. Surprisingly, though, there were few L-29s with the exotic bodywork that adorned so many classics in the twenties and thirties. Most were delivered with the standard Cord sedan, phaeton, or cabriolet body, all of which were also built by Cord-owned companies. Our automobile is the cabriolet model, the same type that was used as the pace car for the 1930 Indianapolis 500.

Cord interiors were luxurious and spacious, up to the standard of a $3,000 automobile in 1929. The dash, though, was more attractive than it was functional. All the gauges were behind little windows, set in two shiny, polished panels. The tiny gauges ahead of the driver were difficult to see at best, while those on the panel facing the passenger were a mystery to the driver. As with several front-drive cars even

The Cord's driveline was so long that a recess had to be cut in the
firewall. A six-foot hood covered the engine.

today, the shift was not the conventional floor-mounted H-pattern, but a push-pull affair sprouting from the middle of the dashboard.

The L-29's performance was not quite up to its looks, with a top speed between 85 and 90 miles per hour. But that really mattered only at cocktail parties and wasn't the reason the likes of John Barrymore, Ronald Colman and Dolores Del Rio bought them. It was the visual effect that counted and the Cord had it.

But even that wasn't enough to carry the L-29 through the Depression. Production was ended in 1932 after only some 4,400 were built. The name Cord then went into limbo until the introduction in 1935 of the coffin-nosed 810 model.

1953 Twin-H Power Hudson Hornet

1953 TWIN-H POWER HUDSON HORNET

Engine Type: L-head in-line 6-cylinder

Displacement: 308 cubic inches (5.0 liters)

Horsepower: 170

Transmission: 3-speed manual

Wheelbase: 124 inches

Overall Length: 208 inches

Overall Height: 60.4 inches

Overall Width: 77.6 inches

The story of the Hudson Hornet begins before America's plunge into the Second World War. In 1941, Hudson's chief body designer, Frank Spring, delivered a prototype car to management for consideration as a new model. It was similar to earlier Hudsons in that it incorporated elements of the company's trademarked "monobilt" construction, a modified unit-body assembly technique that eliminated the heavy sills along the lower body by connecting the body and frame together as a solid unit. But Spring's new car went far beyond the basic "Monobilt" concept. He had moved the body's frame sections to the extreme outside of the car, actually running the rear frame members outside the rear wheels, and because the car's floor was no longer sitting on top of the frame rails, he had dropped the car floor sections to an incredibly close eight inches off the ground. A two-piece driveshaft was used and a hypoid-type rear axle reduced the center hump inside the car and allowed the body and seats to be lowered until the floorboards were the lowest part of the whole car. Called the "step-down" because of the passenger's motion getting into the car, the design was too radical for Hudson's management and the proposal was rejected.

Before Frank Spring, by then a believer in the "step-down" concept, could make another presentation, the United States entered the war. Hudson's Detroit plant stopped producing automobiles and converted to full-scale production of parts for Helldivers, Airacobras, B-29s, and other materials for the war effort. And when the factory returned to auto production in August 1945, with America's postwar economy booming, it was to produce hastily facelifted 1942 models. The market was soon satiated. Frank Spring, sensing the time was right for a fresh design, rescued his rusty "step-down" prototype from the roof, cleaned it up, and again presented it to management.

According to present-day Hudson mythology, management again rejected the design as being "too low" until Hudson President A. E. Barit grudgingly drove the car home from work one night. The prototype's superior handling and roadholding ability—both the result of the car's low center of gravity—are said to have so impressed the conservative and taciturn Barit that he ordered the car into immediate production for the 1948 model year.

Introduced in December 1947, the Hudson Commodore was one of the first new-design postwar cars made in America; the first postwar-design Fords and Chevrolets did not appear until 1949. The Commodore was available with either the company's traditional 254-cubic-inch L-head engine or a 262-cubic-inch engine that produced 121 hp at 4,000 rpm. Either engine was available in a four-door sedan, two-door coupe, or convertible body (all built on a 124-inch wheelbase).

The 1948 Commodore caused quite a sensation when introduced. It was lower than

RETROSPECT

1953 Twin-H Power Hudson Hornet
Owned by Gary J. Kann
Photographed for *Motor Trend* by Mike Parris

the sedans that postwar America was familiar with, standing a mere 60 inches tall at its highest point. And at 75 inches wide, its interior was vast. By 1948 standards, the fastback body looked aerodynamic, low and exciting, with its slab sides, full-skirted rear fenders and narrow gun-slit windows. Backing up the stylists' implied promise of speed was more than adequate performance for a six-passenger family sedan. A Commodore Eight was capable of more than 90 mph top speed, would reach 80 mph in little more than half a minute and, with an overdrive transmission, could nurse 16 miles from a gallon of gasoline.

Performance and styling aside, the feature that really excited the American imagination—the one feature people still remember and talk about nearly 30 years later—is the "step-down" design. Here's the way one person reacted:

> You'd open the door and begin to get into the car. Then it would hit you: My God! You were actually stepping down into this car, not just resting your feet on the top of the chassis, but actually lowering yourself down into the chassis. It was like the difference between lying on a bed and lying in a cradle. It was a very secure feeling.

In 1950, after two years of Commodore production, Hudson added a new model, the Pacemaker, to its line, seemingly as a response to the new low-priced Plymouths, Studebakers, Chevrolets, and Henry J's flooding the market. Although it looked similar to the Commodore series, the Pacemaker was built on a five-inch-shorter wheelbase (119 inches), was more than six inches shorter in overall length (201.5 inches), and was offered with only one engine, a new short-stroke version of the Super Six, displacing 232 cubic inches and producing 112 horsepower. All four of Hudson's transmissions were offered in the Pacemaker as were five different body styles—two-door sedan, four-door sedan, convertible, club coupe, and three-seat business coupe. The new low-price Hudsons sold for $1,675 to $1,795.

Meanwhile, on the medium high price front (the area Hudson aimed for with its Commodore straight eight), the 1949 Oldsmobile was generating great excitement. The 88 and 98 series had brand-new overhead-valve V-8 engines that displaced 303 cubic inches and put out a pavement-shattering 135 horsepower. For a while, it looked like the new Oldsmobile "monkey motion V-8" would break every racing

record in existence and in the process knock Hudson and the other contenders in the medium high price segment of the automotive market right off the map.

This was the beginning of what was to become a fierce industry-wide horsepower race for the next decade and a half. If the overhead-valve V-8 was the wave of the future, as the performance of the 1949–50 Oldsmobiles and Cadillacs seemed to indicate, Hudson needed an almost instantaneous response. That meant they were in deep trouble. The company had spent so much time, effort, and money developing the "step-down" body (tooling alone is said to have cost $18 million) and getting it on the market before any other company's new postwar cars that little attention had been paid to developing new engines. Hudson simply did not have an overhead-valve V-8 waiting in the wings.

So, the company responded in the only way it could—with modification to existing hardware, which produced the Hornet. The post-war L-head Super Six was clearly the best engine in the Hudson stable; it had reliably powered the Commodores and Pacemakers in its 262 and 232-cubic-inch versions and was a basically more rugged and more modern design than the aging 254-cubic-inch eight. The Super Six had full pressure lubrication, in place of the eight's splash oiling. The connecting rod bearings were removable in the six and poured babbitt in the eight. And, most important in an effort to squeeze out more horsepower, the Super Six's crankshaft, connecting rods, and piston pins were larger dimensionally, therefore stronger, than those used in the eight.

By increasing the Super Six's bore to 3-13/16 inches and stretching its stroke to a whopping 4-1/2 inches, Hudson was able to create a 308-cubic-inch six-cylinder engine that exceeded the displacement of even the Oldsmobile V-8 by a few inches. The four-main-bearing engine block was cast of a chrome alloy; the aluminum alloy, cam-ground pistons weighed more than a pound each and were fitted with chrome top piston rings; and each engine was statically balanced before assembly, then dynamically balanced electronically after assembly. This new 145-horsepower engine—significantly 10 horsepower more than the Oldsmobile V-8's output—was to supply the sting for the company's new Hornet model. It was the largest six-cylinder passenger car ever built—and many people believe the finest.

Although nothing more than a facelifted Commodore, the new 1951 Hornet gave the appearance of being an entirely different car. Where the Commodore grille had the flimsy, stuck-on look of an opened venetian blind, the Hornet's twin heavy-chrome grille bars looked like they had grown into place. The downward slope of the chrome grille surround and the inverted crescent-shaped center grille bar pulled the observer's eyes to the outside of the car and toward the ground, giving the whole car a feeling of greater width and a lower profile.

As if to gild the lily, the 1951 Hornet's stylists attached a trapezoidal license plate surround in the center of the front bumper and two diagonal strips of chrome behind it on the leading edge of the grille. Seen from a distance, the license plate surround and grille diagonals work together to defy the observer's depth perception and form a massive chrome triangle smack in the center of the front of the car. At the apex of the triangle's vertical legs is the Hudson logo, an inverted white triangle afloat on a red shield. So you wouldn't forget the symbol of the Hudson Motor Car Company at night, the shield was plastic and illuminated by a small light bulb behind it.

(The triangle is a dominant shape in Hudson history. A triangular shield appeared on the radiator shell of the first Hudson to leave the factory on July 3, 1909. Made of brass, it symbolized the car's three virtues: "Performance, service, and value." It was replaced with a white enameled triangle in 1911 when the company began enameling its cars' radiator shells.)

The stylists in charge of the Commodore-cum-Hornet facelift project must have felt if one triangle is good, more triangles are better, because they went stark raving bonkers over triangles. In addition to the grille and shield, the front end is capped with a hood ornament featuring a big cast triangle. There is a red triangle in the center of each hubcap; the small rear interior lights are triangular; the heater housing under the dashboard is semi-triangular in shape; and even the lowly accelerator pedal comes to a point at the top suggesting—what else?—a triangle.

Part of the advertising copy for the new 1951 Hudson Hornet read, ". . . this high compression engine doesn't have to be luxury-fed on premium gas. It doesn't need to be pampered into top performance. It transforms regular gasoline into the sweetest, fleetest, most flexible going this side of air travel." And to prove how fleet travel by Hornet could be, the company entered NASCAR racing in 1951.

By the end of Hornet's first season, it was in third place among manufacturers, led only by Oldsmobile and Plymouth. These were the days of "pure" NASCAR racing, when the cars on the track had to be "stock," meaning every part of every car had to be available through a dealer. The road to winning lay along the "export" or "police" option route, or in making better equipment available as an optional extra to the public.

Although less powerful than many of the other makes on the NASCAR tracks at the time, the Hornet's lower center of gravity, superior suspension (both front and rear stabilizer bars), and superlative roadholding abilities kept it competitive. Still, the V-8s with new four-barrel carburetors were beginning to give the Hornets a run for their money, so, in June 1952, the factory announced an option it called Twin-H-

Power. Originally investigated in 1937, the Twin-H option included a dual carburetor intake manifold, a pair of Carter WA-1 carburetors and two big air cleaners that filled the engine bay.

From the point of introduction, about half the Hornets sold were equipped with Twin-H-Power. With dual carbs the stock Hornet engine produced up to a reported 170 horsepower, gave the Hornet a top speed of about 100 mph and a 0-60 time of 14 seconds. In the hands of Marshall Teague, a skilled mechanic and one of the top Hudson race drivers of the day, the same car was capable of a top speed of 112 mph. The only modifications made to the "Teaguemobiles" had to do with meticulous engine assembly, machining all parts to the racing clearances allowed by NASCAR, and extremely careful tuning. By the time the 1952 NASCAR season was over, Teague and fellow Hornet drivers Tim Flock, Herb Thomas, Ralph Mundy and Lee Petty had amassed a staggering 27 first-place wins in a total of 34 NASCAR events.

In 1953, Hudson removed the chrome diagonal grille bars from the front of the Hornet and replaced the triangle hood ornament with a phony hood scoop, perhaps an admission they had carried the triangle motif a bit too far. It was, and is, the best-looking Hornet ever built. And with the new 7X racing engine Hudson developed, it was among the fastest Hornets ever built.

Although listed in the Hudson catalogs of the day as a dealer-installed option with the letter designation SU alongside to indicate the engine was meant for the "severe usage" encountered in police work or in export service, the 7X was nothing more than a race modification of the Hornet engine worked out by Hudson engineer Bernie Siegfried, drawing on his Ford flathead racing experience. The basic 308-cubic-inch block was fitted with larger valves, a hotter camshaft, split-exhaust manifold, a cast-iron cylinder head (from the 232-cubic-inch six) machined for a 9.2 to 1 compression ratio and half-inch diameter studs to hold the head gasket in place.

In 1953 Hudson remained NASCAR champion with 22 victories in 34 races thanks to the 7X engine. By 1954, when Hornet wins on the NASCAR circuit dropped to 17, it was obvious to both Hudson and the stock-car racing drivers that the 7X, although the zenith of flathead six-cylinder engine development, was no longer competitive against the new overhead-valve V-8s.

Gary Klann of Riverside, California, owner of the car shown on these pages (and 15 other Hudsons) was first hooked on the 7X engine. He bought it, rebuilt it, and then looked for a body in which to install it. As former president of the California Inland Chapter of the national Hudson, Essex, Terraplane Club, he had little trouble finding the car of his choice. He bought the 1953 Hornet club coupe you see in the pictures from another club member, bolted his 7X engine up to the car's original dual-range Hydra-Matic transmission and promptly put the car in service, towing his other Hudsons back and forth across the country to the national club's annual meets.

The only concession he felt he had to make to automotive progress since 1953 was a set of four 225-by-15-inch radial tires mounted on seven-inch-wide Chrysler wheels. Any further modifications or updating would probably be superfluous. How many "modern" V-8-equipped cars can promise trouble-free service for 60,000 miles or deliver 17 miles per gallon of gas while cruising at 75-85 mph? Gary Klann's 7X-powered 1953 Hornet coupe has done it and at this moment is probably churning up the vast open spaces between Las Vegas and Riverside on his return from yet another national Hudson club meet.

1962 Shelby Cobra 260

1962 SHELBY COBRA 260

Engine Type: overhead valve V-8

Displacement: 289 cubic inches (4.7 liters)

Horsepower: 280

Transmission: 4-speed manual

Wheelbase: 90 inches

Overall Length: 154.5 inches

Overall Height: 49 inches

Overall Width: 65.5 inches

The Cobra was a typical Carroll Shelby exercise. He called one day in March. "Hey, Ah got somethang to show you—c'mon out!" "Out" meant Dean Moon's speed equipment and hubcap emporium where Shelby rented stall and office space for his Goodyear racing tires and himself. And the "somethang" sat in the next-to-last stall on four tautly laced 90-spoke Dunlop wire wheels and next to a dynamometer on which was bolted a small-block Ford V-8 painted with the legend XHP-260.

At first glance the car looked like an unpainted AC Bristol with a longer nose. However, under the hood was the mate to the engine on the dynamometer, XHP-260-1, and squatting in the cockpit was a busy man bolting the shortest driveshaft in captivity between the Borg-Warner four-speed gearbox and a beefy Salisbury rear end center section. The net visual effect was that of a very desirable property that had grown hair in large bundles. The thing hadn't even been fired up, and yet it seemed to sit there growling, gnashing teeth. Not even Shelby knew what he had by the tail at that moment; about all anyone could tell at that point was that whatever it was, it was mean.

What we were looking at was by no means new in 1962. The basic design had been bought by AC Cars from one John Tojeiro nearly ten years before. It had since been seen with the old AC single-cam six and then with the potent Bristol. In this latter form in the late 1950s, it had been an E-Production SCCA Class racer to contend with, virtually owning its class and the one above for five years from 1956 to 1961. At $6,000 it was an expensive device as well, which slowed its sales more than somewhat, considering the simplicity of the machine.

Derived from a one-off racer, the chassis consisted of a pair of large longitudinal frame tubes with one crossmember and two large bridge structures at each end. These bridge structures carried A-arms at the bottom of each end. On top at each end were semi-elliptic transverse springs that also acted as upper control arms for the suspension uprights. The rest of the frame was small diameter tubing whose primary function was to carry the very light aluminum body panels. As indicated, the suspension was fully independent, front and rear. On this particular version there were disc brakes front and rear with the rear discs and calipers carried inboard next to the rear-end section. Later ones were to have the rear discs located outboard because the heat from the brakes augmented the heat in the center section and vice versa, with all sorts of unhappy results.

The cockpit was sparsely covered in fabric and leather and furnished with a pair of superbly comfortable and form-fitting leather-covered seats. On the leather-trimmed dash there was a positive welter of instruments. Though laid in with no particular pattern, there were enough of them to satisfy all but the most crass instrument freak. A medium-sized wood-

RETROSPECT

1962 Shelby Cobra 260 (Number 1)
Owned by Carroll Shelby
Photographed for *Motor Trend* by PPC Photographic

rimmed wheel held an almost vertical position in front of the driver, and on each side of the steering shaft were a pair of antiquated-looking pedals that appeared to have come from a motoring museum. Running down the center of the cockpit was a high central tunnel from which protruded, just below the right rim of the steering wheel, one of the shortest gearshift levers in the memory of racing man. The whole thing was, in short, derived from a racing car and looked it.

The major changes wrought at Shelby's behest were longer springs and A-arms to give a wider track, bigger brakes, a heavier Salisbury center section and drive train, and heavier locating rods to take the added torque. The weight of the A.C. Bristol was about 1,900 pounds and the new Shelby version (no one had come up with the name Cobra at that point) weighed in at 2,100 pounds. The price per pound was down, though, because the list price was $5,995 plus tax and license.

By any standards—today's, those of the muscle-car era of the late '60s, or those of 1962—that car was absolute dynamite. It had style. Totally innocent of paint with the name "Shelby" scrawled in paint on the nose and tail, looking about as raw as a car can look, it still had style, something that made heads turn. Aside from that, it would leave any car on the road standing in its own dents. It had a unique quality that I've seen in few other cars; it got underway in an absolutely blinding rush without any untoward wheelspin or rubber burning, or sideways cop-attracting nonsense. You poked the pedal and dropped the hammer and the result was instant motion forward. The whole thing was a revelation, and while it may have seemed a bit raw and crude to those who were into sophisticated Grand Touring machinery, there was no doubt that this was truly, in every sense of the word, a *sports car*. It was a rolling, moving definition of that much abused and confused term—if you ever need to know what the term means, drive a Cobra.

Shortly after that first session—in which we found that 260 horses from Ford would propel 2,100 pounds of AC roadster at a rate of 150 miles an hour—the car was painted a brilliant pearlescent yellow by Dick Jeffries and went to the New York Automobile Show. There, under the sponsorship of the Ford Motor Company, it stole the show from the rest of the FoMoCo exhibits and those of other companies as well.

The engine in the Cobra One, a small-block Ford V-8, put out 260 horsepower at 5,800 rpm.

Before that spring and summer had ended, two more were worked on with the wars of competition in mind. They were in and out of the shop, back and forth to Riverside and Willow Springs. In the fall, one made its public debut at Riverside in the hands of Billy Kraus. Thanks to a badly designed chamber in a rear hub, the run was short-lived. But while it was running, Billy kept it ahead of the hottest Corvettes on the West Coast. Later that fall, the two cars were taken to Nassau where they demonstrated that they could stay ahead of even the likes of the then-redoubtable Ferrari GTO. One Cobra bid fair to take the Governor's Trophy away from Ferrari until a miscalculation on how much gas a Cobra needed to run for an hour forced a halt to the proceeding.

Cobra Number One, however, was not to join these battles. While others went on to take everything in sight that the SCCA road racers could field, it went back on the street. The pearlescent yellow couldn't take the California sun and turned all leprous looking, so it was exchanged for Guardsman blue, which had become the Shelby team color.

In 1963, the Cobra took home the SCCA B-Production championship. In 1964 they made a run at the Manufacturers' Championship, missed, but took the class in SCCA again. Shelby made a public promise to the effect that ". . . next year, Ferrari's tail is mine."

On July 4, 1965, he made good on his promise. When Bob Bondurant and Jo Schiesser drove a Cobra 289 to win the Grand Touring competition at Rheims, France, clinching the World Championship of Makes for an American manufacturer for the first time, the Cobra rolled into the world's history book. Ol' Shel did indeed build the fastest production car in the world. It's still right up there.

1954 Jaguar XK 120-M

1954 JAGUAR XK 120-M

Engine Type: dual overhead cam in-line 6-cylinder
Displacement: 3.4 liters (207.4 cubic inches)
Horsepower: 160 or 180
Transmission: 4-speed manual
Wheelbase: 102 inches
Overall Length: 173 inches
Overall Height: 51 inches
Overall Width: 63 inches

If ever an automobile deserved the term "landmark car" that automobile is the Jaguar XK 120, which burst onto the scene just after World War II. Until its arrival, a sports car had been a long-hooded, slab-sided roadster with clamshell or cycle fenders and wire wheels—a look once aptly described as a coffin riding on four harps. The XK 120 tore that concept apart, relegating all such cars to the "anachronism" or "classic" category, depending on one's point of view.

In point of fact, the car had not been intended for public consumption. It was only the test bed for a new engine, according to founder and now retired Chairman Sir William Lyons. The clamor of public demand, however, was so great that dies were quickly made for steel bodies and the car was put into production in 1949.

Sir William quickly served notice that the new confection was more than mere looks by sending one over to Belgium to do the now-legendary 132.6 mph blast up and down the Jabbeke-Altre motor highway. It was proof beyond all doubt that the Lyons den had spawned not only the most advanced-looking sports car in the world

but the fastest production sports car in the world as well.

But, electrifying as a car was that could rip off 17-second quarter miles and 10-second zero to sixties (in 1949 when a 25-second quarter was considered brisk) the real shocker was the price. You could land a barebones XK 120 on these shores for a mere $3,345 plus tax and license. (To put that in perspective, a '49 Ford or Chevrolet convertible would get you into hock down at the bank to the tune of $2,500 and change plus tax and license.) It actually shouldn't have been such a surprise, however, since Lyons had long been known for coming up with cars with the "Thousand Pound Look" at prices nearer to the 300 to 400 pounds sterling range.

The immediate result was that the XK 120 became the most desirable and fashionable equipage in the world and particularly in the United States. For Jaguar Cars Ltd. this was fortune of the purest sort, since postwar England was struggling to get solvent again and only those firms with a heavy export trade could get materials priorities. It wasn't long before every spiv and boulevard cruiser who could winkle $2,500 worth of credit out of the bank and come up with the remainder in cash was zooming about the landscape in a Jag roadster and cluttering up the roads for the real enthusiasts. Such a situation wasn't to be borne and something had to be done.

A little over a year after the first introduction, something was done. Chief Engineer William Heynes and enginmeister Wally Hassan came up with a number named the XK 120-M. What the M meant was that you paid about $600 more and got a stiffer ride (to discourage the boulevardiers as much as to augment handling), a pair of camshafts with 3/8 of an inch of lift, pistons with an 8 to 1 compression ratio, a lighter

RETROSPECT

1954 Jaguar XK 120M
Owned by Bruce Carnachan
Photographed for *Motor Trend* by John Lamm

flywheel, dual exhausts, a special crankshaft damper, and wire wheels. The result was that 180 horses lived where 160 lived before. With one of these you could go out and equal the Jabbeke run on any suitable piece of pike if you were so minded.

To celebrate and announce the new M package, Lyons sent chief test driver Norman Dewis back over to Belgium where, in the presence of observers from the Royal Automobile Club of Belgium, he proceeded to better the former record with a two-way average of 140.789 mph. Jaguar in prewar days had never gone in for factory participation in competitive events but they encouraged their customers to do so. With this new weapon their customers went racing for real, all over the world. About the only thing that could touch a 120-M at that point was the then-new and rare Ferrari 166 Barchetta, and for that one had to have real bread, the kind that comes in packets, not just slices. A pair of gentlemen named Leslie Johnson and Bert Hadley actually got their 120-M into third position overall in the 1950 running of Le Mans in the late hours until they went down with a broken clutch.

What you got for your $3,345 was the most advanced production engine in the world for its time, an in-line six-cylinder engine with a fully counterweighted crank in an iron block surmounted by an aluminum dual overhead cam head of the latest design. This was a configuration seen previously only in racing cars and a very few wildly expensive and rare sports and luxury cars such as Bugatti and Alfa-Romeo and others of like but even more rare ilk. As a matter of strict fact it isn't exactly the most common form of engine even to this day, although it lends itself to lowered pollution counts better than any other. As mentioned, this gem developed 160 bhp at 5,000 rpm or 180 bhp at 5,400 rpm—depending on the configuration. In ensuing models, the 140 and 150 series, it was to go up to 210 and 240 bhp and in racing form into the 300 range with very little in the way of real modification.

The engine was set well back in a relatively normal frame albeit of stiffer than usual construction. Up front the suspension was fully independent and, oh wonder, the springing was by torsion bar, a medium just coming into vogue on real racing cars and not to be seen on Chrysler for another six years. At the rear, a pair of relatively soft semi-elliptic springs carried the chassis over a live Salisbury axle. At a time when it was thought that to have good handling a car had to be suspended like a stone boat the Jaguar XK 120 and even the 120-M had what might be considered a decent ride, a bit firm but definitely not hard. It was an enlightening breakthrough, proof that handling was dependent on spring control, not just stiff springing, a fact that our domestic manufacturers sometimes seem not yet to have learned.

One aimed this package with a huge 18-inch steering wheel attached to a Burman recirculating ball steering box that gave approximately three and a bit turns from lock to lock. Stopping was accomplished by means of four 12-inch-diameter Millenite-drummed brakes with the then-impressive 184 square inches of lining area. You could fade them but it took a bit of doing.

Every frosting must have its fingermark and every brew its bug. The Jaguar XK 120 had two notable ones, one of which was one of the most abominable four-speed gearboxes that was ever put into a sports car, crash boxes not excepted. This jewel had the most recalcitrant non-synchronous low gear in the industry. The only way, after it warmed up, to get into low without grinding off a pound of teeth was to slide it into second gear, all the way in, before attempting engagement. Others, even the MG TC, you could touch second gear synchro and then slide into low, but not the Jaguar. This one was an all-the-way proposition. Second gear wasn't all that well synchronized either for that matter and third was only a little better. In short, one didn't speed-shift a Jaguar. The audio effect when a Jaguar driver was in a hurry, especially in racing, was a sort of odd whoom-pa on each shift, up as well as down. This flaw carried right on up through the series to the early XKE.

The other fly in the 120 ointment was its warm nature. To be blunt, the things boiled on the least provocation. It was a common sight after a race in heavy home-going traffic to see the Jags lined up alongside the road with their hoods raised like so many hungry alligators spitting steam. There wasn't much one could do about it until 1955 when the XK 140 came along with an improved water pump, and even then the fix also required one of those auxiliary electric fans. One might be tempted to exchange the four-pound radiator cap for something like an American 15-pound item but that way danger lay. The perils courted by that method were the

The first XK 120 was such a hit at the 1948 London Motor Show that, although intended as a test bed, it was put into production in 1949.

distinct possibility of blowing a head gasket or a freeze plug or both.

But such was the joy of ownership of a 120, particularly a 120-M, that owners put up with these minor problems joyfully, keeping as much as possible away from traffic jams and drag races with dirty-nosed youths in '32 Ford roadsters of the fenderless persuasion. The attachment for many lasts to this day, there being a close-knit group of owners banded together in the Classic Jaguar Association and listed in the XK 120 Register. One such is Bruce Carnachan, a Los Angeles teacher and the owner of the beautiful XK 120-M roadster pictured here. This car is one of the very rare ones that hasn't been restored but rather maintained in that condition since it was first driven away from the dealer. Mr. Carnachan is the second owner and he bought it from a friend, knowing the car from the day the man brought it home. It's the next best thing to buying the car new and being the original owner today. He licked the cooling problem by adding the 140 water pump and an auxiliary fan and then he added the belt to the suspenders by incorporating a coolant recovery system. He has replaced the transmission once but still has the original one, which he is rebuilding. Some added instruments to monitor the engine and new leather are the only other changes. It is still a potent street machine, especially in this day of emissions controls.

"I stayed with a man in a 911-S the other day—surprised myself as well as him," Bruce says with no small amount of pride. You can't ask for much better than that.

1938 Packard 12

1938 PACKARD 12

Engine Type: modified L-head V-12

Displacement: 473 cubic inches (7.7 liters)

Horsepower: 185 (with high compression heads)

Transmission: 3-speed manual

Wheelbase: 139 inches

Overall Length: 231 inches

Overall Height: 71 inches

Overall Width: 74.75 inches

During the luxury boom of the twenties, Cadillac started the V-16 project under the supervision of Owen Nacker. Cadillac needed a serious entry into the elegant automobile category and for it they needed a hook—the V-16. There was (and still is) a luxury in that many cylinders and the speed they hopefully would inject into the huge automobiles, seemed a requirement for a show of wealth. But the V-16 didn't make it to market until 1930, and it wasn't a prime year for luxury automobiles. Although 3,250 V-16 models were sold in the first two years, the bottom fell out, as it did with everything else, in 1932. Only 296 V-16s went out in that year and a mere 125 in 1933. Times went even more sour for the V-16, and only 56 were sold in 1934, another 50 in 1935, and 52 in 1936. They couldn't peddle 50 of them in 1937. Production continued with a new V-16 through 1941, but the sales figures must have had the accountants weeping.

The cheaper Cadillac V-8s and LaSalle models, however, became winners. Their sales decline was stopped in 1934, reversed, and just before the war, Cadillac's total production had jumped to almost 60,000 units.

Why did the V-16 fail? The introduction of the Cadillac V-12, also in 1930, made the V-16 somewhat superfluous luxury. And many claim the bigger engine just didn't have enough power. The dark economic times of the Depression didn't help either. But another major reason was the preeminence of the Packard.

Packard was established in 1899, when the first of James Ward Packard's "anti-Wintons" was built. Packard was so disgusted with the poor quality of a Winton automobile he bought that he decided to build his own.

Like Henry Leyland, Packard was a man who believed in engineering precision and quality. So while the Cadillac was to become one of many cars in a massive corporation, the Packard continued to exist on something of an independent plateau. It remained an automobile of high standard, a point made clear by one-time Packard President Alvan Macauley's motto: "A gentleman's car, built by gentlemen."

Packard's stature as a luxury car was considerable. One Packard author and historian has put that company's share of the 1930 worldwide luxury market at 50 percent—half the pie. It was a deserved reputation, built on elegance and engineering refinement. Untypically, Packards sold well in Europe, then considered by many as the motherland of luxury automobiles.

The Packard V-12 first appeared in 1932 and added proper power performance to the car's image. The smoothness of the V-12 was more fitting than the booming power of a V-8.

Packard bolstered its entire line in 1935 with the smaller "120" models and in 1937, a year when Cadillac recorded sales of 45,223 automobiles, the firm managed to sell 109,518 cars. Packard had the Cadillac—and most other luxury cars—in a corner—at least until the world broke for World War II. However, the V-16

RETROSPECT

1938 Packard 12 All-Weather Cabriolet by Brunn (foreground)
Owned by Phil Hill
1933 Cadillac V-16 Formal Towncar by Fleetwood
Owned by Hillcrest Motor Co.
Photographed for *Motor Trend* by John Lamm

did elevate the Cadillac image, and both the V-12 Cadillac and the V-12 Packard were worthy of the "luxury" designation.

The frame under either the Cadillac or Packard is obviously from another era—with tall frame rails and massive crossmembers. The other mechanical pieces in the chassis look larger than life to home-grown mechanics of the late fifties. Imagine changing the Cadillac's 7.50-by-17 tires with a 1930s jack. Add drag link steering and vacuum-assisted drum brakes, each the size of a large frying pan. The Packard even had vacuum-assist for the clutch. Weighing in at more than three tons, either car makes a modern Thunderbird look like a lightweight.

Remember, this was 35 to 40 years ago, and Cadillac and Packard were already doing a very creditable job of starting, turning, and stopping these gargantuan vehicles. Any modern-day road tester can tell you that the modern luxury cars still don't have that task down pat.

The mechanical attraction, of course, was the many-cylindered engine. The V-8 has been our modern mainstay and the thought of 12 cylinders, much less 16, had been foreign—literally.

The Packard's cylinder banks were separated by 67 degrees and were fed through one downdraft carburetor. Packard opted for a modified L-head instead of the Cad's overhead valves. The camshaft was still set low in the Vee above the crankshaft, but operated directly on the valves through a set-up included in the rocker levers. While the original Packard V-12 was set at 445.5 cubic inches, the bore and stroke by 1938 were 3-7/16 by 4-1/4 inches, providing 473 cubic inches. Horsepower, again with optional high compression heads, was 185, while torque was 430 lbs-ft. at 1,200 rpm. The block was cast iron while both the crankcase and the heads were aluminum.

There was one bit of technological forethought that Cadillac and Packard V-12s shared, "automatic valve silencers." They were hydraulically controlled zero lash mechanisms that eliminated valve noise (a serious consideration in a quiet luxury car) by maintaining zero clearance for the valves. Well before modern hydraulic lifters, these "silencers," located at the push-rod side of the rocker arms, were automatically adjusting valves.

There is a final point to be made about the two cars and that is their body styles. While there are still plenty of chauffeur-driven limousines around, none of them treat the driver with the

Rear seats of the Cadillac V-16 (top) and the Packard 12 (bottom). The gadget in the Packard's right armrest is a radio.

sort of disdain these cars do. And if the deep, set-back rear seats say anything, it is isolation. Settled deep in their armchair comfort, one could drive through a revolution with the window up and hardly notice the disturbance. Why did their owners care to hide, or be hidden? What were they trying to avoid? Perhaps the Depression? The movie stars were seeking protection from their fans, or maybe it was just that this type of automobile was expected of them. No doubt some owners just enjoyed the vehicle for its size and splendor. For others the solid "thump-click" of the door closing was a barrier against the real world.

These automobiles weren't bought for their precise handling, because one didn't drive them in that manner. And when actress Joan Crawford bought this very Cadillac from Hillcrest Cadillac in 1933, it was to comply with a sort of thinking that is probably lost in the "every-man-is-created-equal" world after World War II. That was one of the purposes of that war, remember? Even our largest, most opulent Cadillacs and Lincolns of today are poor, gaudy imitations of that thinking. Compared to silky V-12s and V-16s, even huge 500-cubic-inch engines come across as a bit tacky. They, and 1975 America, miss the attitude that prompted Packard to write in the owner's manual of 1938:

> Public officials who shoulder the responsibility of motor car regulations quite logically look to the better class of drivers to set an example for others. May we, in the interest of all concerned, sincerely request that Packard owners "Always Drive Safely."

Whether we're better off without that sort of thinking is something you'll have to decide for yourself.

1941 Chevrolet Special DeLuxe Coupe

1941 CHEVROLET SPECIAL DELUXE COUPE

Engine Type: L-head in-line 6-cylinder
Displacement: 216 cubic inches (3.5 liters)
Horsepower: 90
Transmission: 3-speed manual
Wheelbase: 116 inches
Overall Length: 195.75 inches
Overall Height: 67.6 inches
Overall Width: 72.1 inches

There's a little of the 1941 Chevrolet in all of us, just as there's a little of the Nebraska farm boy in Johnny Carson, Dick Cavett, and Marlon Brando. The 1941 Chevrolet, in its own tiny way, has had a part in forming our lives. It's a kind of metaphor for what it was to be American in the middle of the twentieth century. What the 1941 Chevrolet says about utilitarian mediocrity, it also says about solid, dependable, predictable Americanism. What it says about the aspirations of the Middle Class to "luxury," it also says about the basic naivete of the American character trying for "a new standard of elegance" on the eve of a catastrophic world war. The 1941 Chevrolet expresses the obtainable dreams of the Middle.

Seemingly every other man, woman, and child who lived through the '40s or '50s owned, rode in, or was intimately touched by a 1941 Chevrolet. If you presently own one you know this is true, because each viewer, father, uncle, or third cousin, has had one "just like this."

For reasons that elude rational analysis, a clean 1941 Chevrolet sitting at an intersection waiting for a light to change has the power to elicit personal confessions of childhood and early adulthood from any and all passers-by. Most of these narratives are of the life-was-grand-then school, but others have a darker side. For instance, one man, in this case a gas station attendant, prefaced his song with the question, "Does this thing have vacuum shift?" It does. There followed a harrowing tale of love and suspense in a Louisiana Bayou early one evening in 1948 during which the complainant found himself crawling in the mud under the car in his high school graduation prom tuxedo trying to get that "son-of-a-pig shifter" into reverse so he could get to the dance, muddied as he was. How did he happen to be out on the Bayou before the dance? "Well, yuh see, I had me this lil' girl that just loved. . . ." There are no private tales where 1941 Chevrolets are concerned. In fact, if a need should ever arise, a 1941 Chevrolet Master DeLuxe Coupe might make an excellent Protestant Confessional.

Chevrolet for 1941 was supposed to be one of those automotive breakthroughs that changes all our lives. It was supposed to convince us once and for all that Detroit knew what was good for us—which apparently they did in 1941. The big model change "bristled" with new mechanical features. The coachwork, featuring "Fisher Unisteel construction, with Turret Top and solid steel underbody" (as opposed to flimsy steel underbody), was considerably different from the previous year. There was extraordinary attention paid to trim detail. While the Nazis were kicking the bejeezus out of Western Europe and those crazy Democrats were trying to pass Lend-Lease, Chevrolet was giving isolationist America "Aristo-Style design," "de luxe Knee-action on all models," "the Chevrolet valve-in-head 'Victory' engine," "Chevrolet's original and exclusive vacuum-power gearshift," and "Safe-

1941 Chevrolet Special De Luxe Coupe Photographed for *Motor Trend*, by John Lamm

T-Special hydraulic brakes." Only the "Victory" engine injected a realistic note. But after all, wouldn't you rather think about the 1941's "thrilling new bigness" than about going to war?

The "Victory" engine was yet another chapter in the endless saga of the Chevy Six. With a 3-1/2-inch bore by 3-3/4-inch stroke, the engine was undersquare, which is typical of its contemporaries. But with a boost in compression ratio to 6.5:1, Chevrolet escalated the horsepower war by 5 to a neck-lashing 90 hp. All this feverish activity was achieved with "lightweight" cast alloy iron electroplated pistons running against babbitt-bearing rods on a four-main-bearing crankshaft. Lubrication was by the old "splash" system used through the early '50s. A single-throat Carter carburetor rammed hearty charges of mixture through this fire-breathing monster, making wheelspin a hazard at all speeds below three miles per hour.

The three-speed synchromesh transmission was conventional enough, but "Chevrolet's exclusive vacuum gearshift" was quite another matter. Power is taken from a vacuum boost cylinder and assists by assuming a claimed 80 percent of the necessary shifting effort. The shift knob is just a flat finger-tip shaped piece of plastic because, when working properly, the vacuum shift allows shifting literally "at a touch of the finger." On the other hand, when the unit isn't working, we suggest two or three strong forearms. Significantly this system remained "exclusive" to Chevrolet. Chevrolet also became exclusive producer of a modification kit that replaced the entire mess with conventional mechanical gubbins. If you have a vacuum shift that works, always smile at it when you open the hood. Get it to like you as a person.

Another wonder for 1941 was Chevrolet's suspension system. No room for convention here! The front had double unequal-length wishbones with coil springs and a trailing stabilizer bar. Ah, but the shocks! They were hydraulic knee-action dampers built into the upper knuckle at the frame. Pretty racy, really. When they were working. But they are now hard to find and their seals are apt to give out, as they did then. If yours work, always smile warmly at them . . . et cetera, et cetera. . . .

The rear suspension was different also. Using regular semi-elliptical springs, shock damping was accomplished with double-acting lever-type units mounted to the frame ahead of the hub and attached to the spring shackle through 90-degree links. Brakes were leading-trailing shoe type, the clutch was diaphragm spring operated, and the air cleaner was in the two-pound Maxwell House Drip Grind school.

As for "Aristo-Style design," what they did was to take a 1940 Chevrolet and make it look more like a loaf of bread. Everything got round and squeezable looking. Red paint was used lavishly to highlight the chrome (actually mostly stainless steel) trim and the result was quite handsome. Red pinstripes on the grille bars, wheels, and side moulding combine with red and blue trim on the hubcaps and Chevrolet medallions to give the car a very bright color-coordinated appearance. Late 1941 Special DeLuxe models also offered "shark tooth" wheel trim rings with red "teeth" around their circumference and chrome fender mouldings. Trim and interior differed in detail between Special DeLuxe and Master DeLuxe models. The Special had stainless steel mouldings around exterior windows and at the body crease line, a wider trim strip incorporating the hood vents, wood-grain dash, clock, and special two-spoke steering wheel. Two-tone Bedford cord upholstery was also an option in the Special DeLuxe. At midyear a flying lady hood ornament and special front bumper override bars were made available on all models.

The 1941 line of Chevrolets offered in Special DeLuxe were the Town Sedan (two-door sedan), Five-Passenger and Business Coupes (the latter without a rear seat), Sport Sedan (four door), Station Wagon, and Cabriolet. The Station Wagon had beautifully sculpted ash and mahogany siding with the spare tire incorporated into the tailgate. The Cabriolet offered a vacuum-operated top-retracting mechanism. The Master DeLuxe models were the Sport Sedan, Town Sedan, and Five Passenger and Business Coupes. All models had no-draft ventipanes and double interlocking hood releases, one of these under the dash to "insure that the hood cannot be opened accidentally or by unauthorized persons." You can't be too careful.

Judging from the surprising number of '41 Chevrolets still around, the car was a success both mechanically and financially. Chevrolet had been sales leader for nine of the previous ten years and 1941 made it 10 of 11. They struck a balance between economy and pretension to

A wood-grain dash and two-spoke steering wheel were special marks of luxury in the 1941 DeLuxe Coupe.

The styling differences between the 1940 Chevrolet and the 1941 Special DeLuxe Coupe (background) were not so sweeping as ads of the time indicated.

elegance, between dependability and mechanical innovation, and between tradition and modernity that made this car the standard of 1941 in the Middle Class. It was also, for more macabre reasons, the standard American car for the next four years. And in an age of gas rationing and extreme rubber shortages, a simple reliable 55-mile-an-hour car was precisely what America had to have. Yes, you could go faster if you'd just siphoned some gas or stolen some tires. But for the rest of America it was just slow drives on Sunday afternoons waiting to hear news from Salerno. It's still that kind of car, a car for Americans to live through their crises in. Maybe that's why people are induced to tell their life's story at the mere sight of a nice 1941 Chevrolet. It has a reassuring ability, regardless of the constant comings and goings of more expensive and faster luxury cars, simply to endure.

1957 Porsche 356A Speedster

1957 PORSCHE 356A SPEEDSTER

Engine Type: overhead valve opposed 4-cylinder

Displacement: 1.6 liters (97 cubic inches)

Horsepower: 75

Transmission: 4-speed manual

Wheelbase: 83 inches

Overall Length: 155.5 inches

Overall Height: 46 inches

Overall Width: 65.3 inches

Perhaps the most difficult aspect of writing about old automobiles is trying to re-create the subject car's era for the reader—imagining the first decade of the century with its deeply rutted roads, the second ten years with World War I, the expansive twenties, and the deflated thirties. This problem is not so pronounced, however, for the Porsche, because its history does not go back too far. If you celebrated your twenty-fifth birthday in 1974, you are as old as this already legendary company.

For Dr. Ferdinand Porsche's personal accomplishments, you do have to go back further. His first car design was an electric buggy for Jakob Lohner and Company, and it won a grand prize at the 1900 Universal Exposition in Paris. This design was followed by a mind-boggling array of others: Austro-Daimlers, World War I mortars, the Mercedes-Benz SSKL, Wanderer automobiles, Auto Union Grand Prix racers, speed records cars, World War II tanks, and, of course, the Volkswagen.

Projects such as the tanks landed the 72-year-old designer in an unheated French jail after the war. He was ransomed with money raised in a

contract with Italian Piero Dusio to build the fascinating, but ill-fated, Cisitalia Grand Prix car. This racer featured the first Porsche baulk-ring synchromesh transmission, and the driver had a choice of two- or four-wheel drive.

However, in the few years between Porsche's release and his death in January 1951, there was an even more important project to be launched. It started rather shakily in the Corinthian village of Gmund in Austria. The country was still occupied by foreign troops and the local money was virtually worthless. The Dusio project had withered financially, and, quite frankly, the Porsche firm was out of work. Therefore, Porsche's son, Ferry, fell back on Project 356, a two-place sports car based on the Volkswagen. (All Porsches are named by their project number. The early Porsches were based on project 356; the present ones are from projects 911 and 914.)

The Porsches had to scrounge pieces for the first car, a mid-engined convertible, but work started in late 1947. By early summer in 1948, the prototype was being test-driven over local mountain roads. Apparently the design worked from the start. The secret was weight, just 1,300 pounds—little enough that even the slightly modified VW engine gave sporting performance.

The press began to report the progress of the newest Porsche project, and the response was encouraging. On that basis, Ferry Porsche decided to go ahead with the rear-engined coupe version, so work started on what are now called "the Gmund cars." That original set eventually numbered 50—45 coupes and 5 roadsters. They were all aluminum-bodied, a feature that made them prime racing cars.

Porsche was hampered, however, by its Austrian location; the company had to return to

RETROSPECT

1957 Porsche 356A Speedster
Owned by Chuck Cooper
Photographed for *Motor Trend* by John Lamm

Germany if production of the sports car was to be a serious venture. Not only had Dr. Porsche been forbidden to return to Germany, but also his factory at Stuttgart was occupied by the U.S. Army, which would not leave until 1956. Therefore, the Porsches contracted with Reutter, a coachworks that had done prewar work for them, to build steel bodies for the next production run. It was further arranged that Reutter would set aside a portion of their Stuttgart factory grounds for final assembly of the cars. There, in a set of wooden huts, the modern Porsche company finally was established. (Years later, Porsche would buy Reutter.)

Porsche's first year of serious production was 1950. In 1949, one of the Gmund cars had been shown at the Geneva show, and orders piled up. The first steel 356 models, produced as both coupes and cabriolets, continued to share many Volkswagen pieces. However, the Porsche version of the opposed four-cylinder engine, which put out a meager 40 horsepower, was a bit smaller than the VW version (1086cc versus 1131 cc). With the high price and low availability of gasoline, mileage counted as well as power, so this was not a drawback.

The dimensions of the 356 remained basically unchanged for 15 years. In 1953, the car was treated to a minor face lift, and additional mechanical changes justified the model designation 356A in 1956. In 1960, a gentle restyling gave the car more graceful, rounded lines and brought about the label 356B; then, three years later, the 356C with four-wheel disc brakes was introduced. The 356C completed the line, and the 911-912 models came along in 1965.

In comparison with the dramatic annual styling changes coming out of Detroit, the variations in Porsche models seem fairly simple. Of course, any serious Porschist can go on for hours about the minor differences—the one-piece windshield after 1953, the twin rear grilles added in 1962, and the short-term "Continental" and "America" models. However, for the average observer of sports cars, Porsche models are easily divided into the early and late 356 models, the 911-912, and the return to mid-engined cars with the 914.

It isn't that easy to classify the engines. While five different displacement engines were used in the 356 series, there were 12 variations all together, due to variations in horsepower and torque. This is to say nothing of the minor engine differences, such as those that occurred in the bearings and carburetor, in the number of crank case sections and rings.

Among the Porsches was a model that has become one of the most desirable—the Speedster. It was built from autumn 1954 until 1958. The car, originally meant only for export to the United States, specifically to California, was rather spartan. It suffered from an obvious lack of weatherproofing, including a light top that was always flapping and side curtains that leaked when it rained. And in an era when American car suspensions were discussed in terms more appropriate to the description of marshmallows, the close-coupled Porsche was a revelation to many drivers. But the absence of amenities such as side window glass contributed to the Speedster's light weight, 130 pounds less than the standard Porsche models. Sold with the 1500cc or 1600cc engine (not 1.5 or 1.6 liters—use "cc" when referring to early Porsches), they bombed through the mid-fifties. Most road tests of the era put Speedsters' 0 to 60 mph times in the 10-13 second bracket and clocked their top speeds at just over 100 mph, depending on which engine was fitted. (That is about what a 1975 model of the 262-cubic-inch Chevrolet Monza V-8 can do.) To this day, there are Speedsters winning Sports Car Club of America races.

Speedsters gave more than speed, however. They were attractive enough that they sold eventually almost everywhere, even in intemperate climates. Something about the squat windshield and smooth inverted saucer lines still attracts people to the Speedster—even people over six feet tall, who have to crouch to drive one. Today, as a result, a concours example costs between seven and nine thousand dollars.

While older Porsches have been playthings, their status is changing, particularly since the introduction of the 911 models. With the trend spurred by the increasing cost of new Porsches and the increasing numbers of collectors in search of well-preserved older cars, vintage 356s are making the transition from "car" to "collector's item."

Joel Naive, who lives just north of San Diego, California, may profit from this change in Porsche status. He restores Porsches for the fun of it. His black 1950 356 coupe (shown with this story) has been subjected to the same sort of pick-it-apart-and-rebuild-it restoration that was once reserved for Duesenbergs and Bugattis.

1950 Porsche, owned and restored by Joel Naive.

In 1950, the Porsche was powered by a slightly modified
Volkswagen engine.

The slots in the screw heads have even been aligned. Next to the 356 in Naive's garage is his 550 Spyder, stripped, sanded, and in primer. The car's overhead camshaft Carrera engine is on a cart and the wiring harness is neatly laid out on a sheet of plywood. Both cars are better than banked money right now, the value of each as high as the spirits of the next man who feels he must own them.

But drivers' loyalty to their Speedsters is not based on looks and speed alone. For instance, the car shown on the preceding pages, owned by Chuck Cooper, has had little more than gasoline, oil, wash water, and wax since 1957. That's over 80,000 miles with the same reliable "r-r-r-u-u-u-m-m-m." Though it would be incorrect to call the Speedster's engine a VW model (purists in particular, would rip your heart out), the close relationship has given the Speedster obvious advantages, including excellent fuel mileage and legendary durability. When Dr. Ferry Porsche was told there were no Porsches in the Harrah Automobile Collection in Reno, Nevada, he commented that it was probably because they were all still on the road.

That, of course, is where they belong.

1927 Bugatti Royale

1927 BUGATTI ROYALE

Engine Type: single overhead cam in-line 8-cylinder
Displacement: 12.7 liters (778 cubic inches)
Horsepower: 275-300
Transmission: 3-speed manual
Wheelbase: 170 inches
Overall Length: 228 inches
Overall Height: 70.5 inches
Overall Width: 78.5 inches

As early as 1913, there were indications Ettore Bugatti had in mind plans to build a car that would outdo the Rolls-Royce, already the darling of the wealthy. Development work on the engine had already started when World War I refocused Bugatti's energies on "aero engines." Some think it was best, as Bugatti's war experiences helped to hone more finely his self-taught engineering. So it wasn't until the mid-twenties that the Type 41, as the Royale was officially tagged, was readied for production.

The Type 41's size was a paradox. If you remember the Type 37A, you'll recall that Bugatti's race cars were successful because he built small, light racers that could out-scoot the monster machines. But the Royales were anything but small and light. Production wheelbase settled at 169 inches (one source claims 170 inches), while the weight, depending on the body fitted, varied between 3-1/2 and 4 tons.

The frame would have been a credit to any bridge builder. It had side sections as deep as 10 inches with seven hefty, tubular crossmembers tying them together. The rear axle was suspended by the traditional Bugatti quarter elliptic springs, which were backed up by a second set to help cover the wide weight range the chassis would be expected to support. (Remember, with a fuel capacity of 30 Imperial gallons or more, a full tank added the weight of one very rotund gentleman.) And the car was designed with the potential to support coachwork that accommodated seven to nine passengers.

The tubular front axle was similar to those on Bugatti's racing cars. It was effective and neatly constructed. First a solid, forged rod was bored from end to end; then the extremities were hammered solid. It was heated and shaped, resulting in a one-piece axle, solid at the ends but hollow in the middle.

Brakes continued another Bugatti tradition. They were mechanically operated. But unlike the "press-and-pray" binders of the mid-thirties, the Royale's cable-operated system is said to work very nicely, and no Royale has ever been known to crash because of faulty brakes. Between the manual brakes and heavy steering, though, the Royale (sometimes called the "Golden Bugatti") was no lady's car.

Of course, one doesn't move an automobile the size of the Royale with any ordinary engine. Bugatti had plenty of room under the hood and the straight-eight he designed fit nicely. It was 55 inches long, weighed 770 pounds, and displaced 784 cubic inches. Unlike modern powerplants, which are really an assemblage of pieces, the Royale's engine seemed hewn from a solid block of steel, Like other Bugatti engines, there was no detachable head and the overhead cam bobbed up and down, working right through the top of the engine. Massive water jackets covered the outside of the engine right down to crankshaft level, meaning a valve job required pulling the engine, bottom end, every-

RETROSPECT

1927 Bugatti Royale
Owned by The Briggs Cunningham Museum
Photographed for *Motor Trend* by John Lamm

thing. But then, if you couldn't afford the service. . . .

The pistons and rods appeared conventional in form, though any piece built to zero tolerance is certainly not conventional. The crankshaft and camshaft were a bit more involved. Both were machined in two pieces, then bolted together. The crankshaft spun in nine water-cooled main bearings.

Each cylinder had three valves, "two admissions, one exhaust," another Bugatti trademark. Two plugs were used in each cylinder, one sparked by coil, the other by magneto. The mixture they fired was inhaled through a large, one-barrel carburetor of Bugatti design. The explosions weren't in very rapid succession because you don't send 4.9-inch pistons running up and down a 5.1-inch bore too quickly. The motor did churn out 275-300 horsepower, but it was no "revver" with that output coming between 1,700-1,800 rpm. But Lord, just imagine the torque.

A healthy twist is needed to start more than 3-1/2 tons rolling, so the three-speed transmission had an extra-low "emergency" first gear. Second was actually direct drive, normally used for around-town work. Third gear was an overdrive, but not in the 1974 fuel economy sense. It was, rather, for fast running. Experienced Royale drivers (how many can there be?) say the torque was so great, one could pull away from 3 miles per hour in top gear, a favorite Bugatti demonstration trick.

The Royale's top speed is a question of "Who Do You Trust?" Most estimates put it in excess of 100 miles per hour. Best of all answers came in a factory data sheet, which claimed, "The car will attain any speed desired by the designer." Enough said.

All that gear multiplication wasn't happening in a conventional gearbox, but in the Royale's huge transaxle. The power spun directly out of the engine through two heavy fabric universal joints into the two-plate wet clutch, housed just below the driver (it whirled in a combination of light oil and paraffin). Generator and starter motor were mounted on the aluminum clutch case. A short shaft then ran the power back to the combination transmission/rear axle.

The tall cast aluminum wheels, along with the horseshoe-shaped radiator, were the one basic design link in all the Royales. And it was a beautiful carryover. The broad flat surfaces

were detailed at the edge with a line of delicate brake-cooling vents. Originally, the British tire firm Rapson built special four-ply 36 x 6.75-inch tires for the cars, but successive owners have had to make do with whatever they could stretch over the rims, from gun carriage tires to tractor tires with hand-cut treads.

There were only six Royales built, although some experts claim seven Royale chassis had been manufactured, with one still in hiding or destroyed. Of the six known to have been constructed, two men own a pair apiece.

As a point of interest, the first Royale engine

John Burgess of the Cunningham Museum is shown behind the
steering wheel of the museum's Royale.

The Bugatti Royale's engine was 55 inches long, weighed 770
pounds, and churned out 275-300 horsepower—between 1,700
and 1,800 rpm.

was not installed in a Royale chassis, but in that of a Packard. Royale No. 1 (chassis no. 41,100) was first seen in 1927, with a Packard touring car body (perhaps off the chassis just mentioned). It was also reputed to have a 14.7-liter engine (869 cubic inches). The Packard was the first of five bodies that would grace this chassis. The second was a closed, two-seat body shown on the car at the 1928 Paris Salon. A four-door double brougham, with oval opera window that would be the envy of any Detroit design studio, was next up. It was followed by a concours-winning, four-window coupe body by Weymann. After Bugatti personally crashed 41,100, its final wrappings were added, a coupe de ville body by Le Patron's son Jean. The car was one of the three Royales held by the Bugatti family until after World War II, until, at the end of the sixties, it was sold to M. Fritz Schlumpt, a French industrialist and enthusiast extraordinaire who collects Bugattis like some men collect stamps.

1911 Regal Underslung

1911 REGAL UNDERSLUNG

Engine Type: L-head in-line 4-cylinder

Displacement: 184.3 cubic inches (3.2 liters)

Horsepower: 20-25

Transmission: 3-speed manual

Wheelbase: 106 inches

Overall Length: 142 inches

Overall Height: 73 inches

Overall Width: 64 inches

It has been fifty-five years since the last Regal was pushed off the assembly line in Detroit. There was no panic in 1920 at the thought of an automobile company going under. The economic weeding-out process that has left us with only four major auto makers today was then eliminating early manufacturers by the dozen. Most, like the Boss, the Darby, the Johnson and the Pittsburgh, died anonymously. Others, often on the strengths of one model, are remembered.

Regal might still have joined the ranks of the forgotten were it not for their Underslung models. With their chassis so low to the ground, the Underslungs of 1911 looked like Porsches among Cadillacs today. Regal wasn't the first company to use the underslung principle, the American Motor Car Co. having started it in 1907. But the American Underslungs were expensive and heavy, where the Regals were $900 . . . and quick. To some they were the "poor man's Mercer." But let a 1911 issue of *Cycle and Automobile Trade Journal* explain the Regal Underslung in the writing style of the era:

The season of 1911 finds the Regal Motor Car Co. of Detroit offering three distinct models, the Regal "30" a pioneer in the medium price field, and which has proved so uniformly satisfactory, a "40," seven-passenger touring car following closely the "30" lines, save that it is larger and more powerful, and the "20" a brand new two-passenger roadster, giving a line sufficiently comprehensive to meet practically every requirement. . . .

In this connection a word regarding the factory development of the Regal Company might not prove amiss, no other automobile concerning Detroit having undergone more extensive changes in the same period. It is only more than a year ago that the Regal offices and shops were crowded into an unpretentious building where sufficient space in which to properly handle the business was at a premium. Now there is a large four-story office building, a factory building 600 feet long and 200 feet wide, and two stories high, with the most modern equipment, and seven other buildings which, together with a one-fifth mile testing track, cover nearly two city blocks.

Of the three models offered by the Regal Company perhaps the greatest interest centers in the Model N, as the "20" Roadster is designated, this being an entirely new car, and marking an invasion of consequence in the low-priced realm, the Roadster with complete equipment selling at $900.

Outwardly the Model N is of very pleasing design, the principal departure from conventional lines being found in the underslung frame, the weight being carried below instead of above the axles. This gives a rakish effect, and at the same time provides for any road conditions that may be encountered, the actual clearance being ten inches. There is a roomy double seat, with plenty of space at the rear for a fifteen gallon gasoline tank and a box [trunk] of liberal dimensions. The fenders are long and sweeping in design, and with the 32-inch wheels give the car a racy appearance.

Although incorporating many of those features which have made the Regal "30" such a success, the "20" power plant marks a considerable departure from its predecessor. The cylin-

RETROSPECT

1911 Regal Underslung Roadster
Owned by Hillcrest Cadillac
Photographed for *Motor Trend* by John Lamm

ders, four in number, are of best quality gray iron, cast en bloc instead of in pairs. They have a 3-3/4-inch bore and a 1-1/2-inch stroke, the motor developing 20-25 h.p. All valves are on the left side, and are actuated from a single cam shaft made from a one-piece steel forging, with the cams and time gear flange forged integral. The time gears are of liberal size, with spiral teeth, affording absolute quietness in operation. The cam shaft runs on three bronze bearings, provision being made for taking up any end play.

The crank case is barrel type, of cast iron, with end bearings carried on separate castings. The crank shaft is of two-bearing type, 2-1/2 inches in diameter, die forged from special heat-treated steel, all bearing surfaces being accurately ground to size, and shaft and flywheel carefully balanced, extra large sleeve bearings are provided, and the matter of lubrication has been taken care of in an efficient manner. Inside the crank case, just over the bearings, pockets are provided to catch the oil, ducts from these pockets lead to the bearings, and they give a plentiful supply at times.

Connecting rods are of dropped forged I beam section, of high-grade steel, their bearings being die cast composition, made in halves and scraped to give an accurate bearing surface. The main engine journals are solid bushings of special white metal alloy, die cast under pressure.

Lubrication is by a forced circulating system, the oil being drawn by a gear driven pump from a reservoir in the bottom of the crank case through special tubes and ducts to the different bearings and connecting rods, a positive stream of oil being supplied at all times to each part needing lubrication. The unused oil running back to the bottom of the crank case proper, overflows into the oil reservoir, and from there is again pumped to the different bearings.

Cooling is by means of a patent thermal system, which eliminates all pumps, a radiator of exceptional size, and a belt-driven fan mounted on a bracket directly in front of the motor, and which insures ample circulation of air through the radiator and around the engine. Adjustment of the belt is made through a set screw in the tubular standard by means of which the fan may be raised or lowered, as the belt requires, while its location may be altered horizontally by means of a threaded shaft.

Ignition is provided by a dual system, including a high tension magneto with distributor and single non-vibrating coil on the inside of the dash. The magneto is a part of the standard equipment. It is located at the left side of the motor, well toward the rear, and is driven from the time gear shaft, all gears being enclosed. A set of dry batteries is provided for starting, and a double-throw kick switch is located on the dash.

An interesting illustration of the attention bestowed on details is furnished in connection with the ignition system. Instead of carrying the wires loose, as is a common practice, they are conveyed through a T-shaped section of tubing securely supported by uprights anchored to clamps holding the inlet and exhaust manifolds. This gives a more sightly appearance, and affords protection to the wiring system.

Accessibility is one of the noticeable features of the "20" power plant. All gears are located at the front of the motor in such a manner that by removing the forward half of the case in which they are housed they are laid bare for inspection or adjustment. The valves are all within easy reach for adjustment, and may be readily removed when grinding becomes necessary. Exhaust ports and manifolds, as well as inlets, are located at the left side of the motor, and the latter may be removed by loosening clamps. The magneto is easily accessible upon raising the left side of the hood, as is also the oil pump.

The clutch employed on the Regal "20" is a very efficient example of cone type, leather faced with spring insert, which gives easy but positive action, with a noticeable freedom from jerking or slipping. Three coil springs, so fitted that they can readily be adjusted, hold the clutch in engagement.

From the clutch power is transmitted direct through a single universal joint and driveshaft to the transmission, which is of selective sliding gear type, with three speeds forward and reverse, the driving shaft being enclosed in a propeller tube which also acts as a torsion tube.

In accordance with Regal practice, an arrangement, by the way, that has proved eminently satisfactory, the transmission on the model N is combined with the rear axle housing, giving a unit construction that assures correct relative position of the gears whatever conditions may be encountered. The gears are heat-treated nickel steel, and a positive interlocking mechanism makes it impossible to have more than one set of gears in mesh at the same time, thus eliminating the danger of stripping through carelessness or confusion. The entire transmission runs on Hyatt high-duty roller bearings, transmission and axle gears running in a bath of oil which gives plenty of lubrication at all times.

In keeping with the Regal principle, the rear axle is of semi-floating type, very substantially made, having a truss rod, and with the axle shafts mounted on Hyatt roller bearings.

The front axle is of I-beam type, dropped slightly in the middle, with spring seats forged integral. In keeping with the rest of the car, this axle is made sufficiently strong to withstand any strain to which it may be subjected. Cup and cone bearings are employed, and the knuckle pins and spindles are liberally proportioned.

The steering mechanism is of worm and gear type, easy in action, absolutely irreversible, with the knuckles placed forward of the front

The engine developed 25 horsepower and ran very quietly.

axle. The frame of the "20" is pressed channel secion steel, full underslung, with a sharp upsweep at either end, which, with semi-elliptic springs both front and rear, brings the body of the car well below the accustomed level, although providing plenty of clearance. The entire power plant, including the control system, is mounted on a tubular subframe.

Two sets of brakes are provided, both acting directly on the hub drums, and giving perfect control in this quarter. Wheels are of artillery type, each having twelve 1-1/4-inch spokes, and are fitted with 32 x 3-inch tires. The car has a 100-inch wheel base.

The body is of side door roadster type, which, with a long hood, rakish fenders, steering column and gasoline tank at rear of driver's seat provides a racy looking little machine. With standard equipment the Regal "20" sells at $900.

1931 Chrysler CG Custom Imperial Le Baron Sports Roadster

**1931 CHRYSLER CG CUSTOM IMPERIAL
LE BARON SPORTS ROADSTER**

Engine Type: L-head in-line 8-cylinder

Displacement: 384.8 cubic inches (6.3 liters)

Horsepower: 135

Transmission: 4-speed manual

Wheelbase: 145 inches

Overall Length: 217 inches

Overall Height: 59.5 inches

Overall Width: 73 inches

It looks something like the Queen Mother of all T-series MGs, but it's as American as bathtub gin. It's a Chrysler CG Custom Imperial Le Baron Sports Roadster, a set of wheels worthy of any Scott Fitzgerald movie. And a raccoon coat and a hip flask would have been right in style on the icy, gray, winter day we tested the big, red hunk on the freeways of the San Francisco Peninsula.

The car, you see, was an anachronism the day it rolled out the factory door in 1931. In '31, Prohibition's rotgut breath still wafted over the land, right enough, but the citizenry needed a drink as never before. Echoes of the stock market crash reverberated in Wall Street and the shock waves were still spreading. Herbert Hoover fretted in the White House as the world hurtled down the rocky slide to the Great Depression.

Walter Percy Chrysler surely picked one helluva time for his then seven-year-old company to introduce a new luxury car, didn't he? To top it off, the Imperial series wasn't exactly an engineering tour de force. Chryslers had all along had such technical niceties as four-wheel hydraulic brakes and high compression engines. Chryslers had even raced with distinction, as they say, at such speed spas as Le Mans and in the twenty-four-hour Belgian Grand Prix. (They finished third and fourth behind a Bentley and a Stutz in France and two weeks later placed second, third, and sixth at Spa.)

For all that, the '31 Imperial's chief mechanical claim to fame was a straight eight engine that displaced almost 385 cu. in. This was a first for Chrysler, to be sure, but hardly a high water mark in the American auto industry. (Others of its peers in the domestic luxury field offered vee-type engines of up to sixteen cylinders.) Not that the Chrysler eight couldn't get the job done. In its "Red-Head" version, that 6-liter, L-head anchor up front could get the 5,000-pound car moving faster than 100 mph. It still can. Besides, eight cylinders were enough for conservative Walter Chrysler and that, by God, was that!

Styling is what makes Doug O'Connell's king-sized sports car the "elegant straight eight" that a whiskey company calls it. Executed to order by Le Baron, then a genuine coachbuilder, not just a corporate nameplate, it epitomizes what old-car buffs classify as the Classic Era. Its swoopy fenders, long hood, low silhouette, and generally rakish air give no hint that Chrysler then was only four years away from the lumpy Airflow.

Doug O'Connell says his Roadster was among 50 that were handcrafted by Le Baron on the Imperial chassis in 1931 and, as far as he knows, is one of only five still in existence. His is far and away the most widely known.

Shortly after O'Connell completed the fifteen-month restoration of his car almost fourteen years ago, he took it on the *concours d'elegance* circuit. It won everything in sight, including the Best of Show at prestigious Pebble Beach. Shell

Oil featured the car in its television advertising in 1961 and Minnesota Mining and Mineral cranked out its image on thousands of calendars. *Car Life* published an article and road test in its May 1961 issue.

O'Connell contends that it also is the best, superior even to museum owner Bill Harrah's example in Reno. "Harrah's car doesn't even have the right bumpers," he confides, adding that it currently is being re-restored and "I hope they're doing a better job this time."

O'Connell did all of the restoration, except the upholstery and top, himself. It has stood up well, considering that the car is in almost daily use. "I drive it whenever there is a place to park inside or where I can keep an eye on it," he said. "You know, people just can't leave an old car like it alone. They climb all over it and pull off parts."

Bet he doesn't drive it in the rain though. I saw no sign of the side curtains, which must have been made of isinglass.

O'Connell's fascination with man's mechanical conveyances goes back to the mid-1930s in his native Chicago when he mastered the now vanished craft of all-around auto mechanic. "We specialized in big prestige autos," he recalled. "The ones other mechanics wouldn't work on because they were too complicated and strange." He name-drops Isotta-Fraschini and a Minerva, complete with armed chauffeur and footman, but there is no doubt about his true love. "Chrysler was my preference," he declares, "because of their durability and the engineering in their chassis and running gear. Chrysler actually goes too far in its engineering."

The engineering detail is a Chrysler trademark, maybe the result of Chrysler's first mechanical experience, working as a door-to-door salesman and janitor before he became plant manager for the American Locomotive Company. He switched to the auto industry as plant manager of General Motors' Buick Division and rose to Buick president and general manager before storming out in a huff in 1919 after a series of clashes over policy with GM chief executive Will Durant. Chrysler subsequently overhauled the dying Willys-Overland operation and converted a similar salvage job for Maxwell-Chalmers into the Chrysler Corporation.

Driving O'Connell's CG Roadster proved his point about the car's engineering. Despite being the product of a time when wheels were attached to solid, no-nonsense axles and springs were fore-and-aft leaves, the car has a ride vastly superior to many modern sports cars, especially those of English manufacture. This is at least partly due to its 145-inch wheelbase and battleship solidity. (In describing what he wanted in the cars that bore his name, Chrysler told his engineering triumvirate of Carl Breer, Owen R. Skelton, and Fred M. Zeder that they should pursue "the power of a super-dreadnought, but with the speed and endurance of a fleet scout cruiser.") That '31 Roadster certainly fits the specifications.

It dwarfs the modern Imperial with which it shares the two-car garage of O'Connell's modest home in Mountain View, California. Yet it is so well proportioned that off by itself it doesn't look all that big.

The engine came to life with no particular fuss, despite the chilly weather. The smog-controlled products of Big Brotherism should do half as well. All eight of those big cylinders were readily apparent and definitely individualist until they got comfortably warm. Then the engine ran with a smoothness largely forgotten in the Age of the V-8.

Its impressive dimensions notwithstanding, the CG Roadster has a tiny passenger compartment and a squinty little windshield, both owing more than a little to the open-cockpit biplanes of its time. There is, however, a rumble seat. Leather-padded coaming stretches all the way around. The controls are mansized and fall readily to hand, in the accustomed phrase of car testers. They could hardly do otherwise in the space allotted the driver. An altimeter is included as standard equipment.

Power steering was not a regular option in 1931, so the hefty steering wheel is bellybutton close for leverage at low speed.

The car's only handling vice is a very determined self-centering action in the steering. It damn well lets you know that the front wheels would much rather go straight ahead than around corners. If your arms hold out though, enough lateral G-load can be generated to shift you sideways on the bench-type seat.

All in all, the CG Roadster is an honest, if technically uninspired, piece of machinery. Its main allure is visual. Every fitting is a work of meticulous craftsmanship and the whole car is over-engineered, just like the locomotive with which Chrysler got his first mechanical experience.

The '31 Roadster is at its best on freeways,

although it was constructed before the concept was even conceived. With only 135 hp and 2-1/2. tons to move, acceleration is somewhat short, coming into its own at 70 mph. It tracks, really, as if it were on rails. (Thanks, American Locomotive.) The steering, once in motion, is light and precise. There is a definite tendency to let the speedometer creep toward the 100 mph calibration. There are four speeds in the transmission, but low is a compound stumppuller and only the top three are ever needed.

O'Connell says he and his wife, Lea, think nothing of taking the 41-year-old car on a 4-hour run to Reno, Nevada, about 350 miles away across the towering Sierra Nevadas. Why Reno? Harrah's car collection, that's why.

He also is talking about another workover for the CG Roadster. A perfectionist might concur. There are, after all, a couple of small fatigue cracks in the metal at the corners of the rumbleseat and touches of deterioration on the nickel-plate windshield brackets.

Even if O'Connell puts the car back in concours condition, though, it won't see the show circuit again. He objects bitterly to the present emphasis on white-glove cleanliness and brightwork at the expense of function and originality. And he would in no way stop driving the car just to win a few more trophies. However, O'Connell seldom misses a parade.

"We love the car," he admitted over a cup of instant coffee in the breakfast nook of their home. "Sometimes I think I get boring talking about it."

But O'Connell also told me about a dentist in the far northern California town of Redding for whom he restored a 1932 Chrysler Phaeton. "He couldn't think of anything else," O'Connell recalled. "I finally told him to get rid of it. It was becoming an obsession."

Pretty strange advice, coming from the man who has got to be the biggest Imperial fanatic since old Walter P. himself.

1930 Cadillac V-16 Roadster

1930 CADILLAC V-16 ROADSTER

Engine Type: overhead valve V-16

Displacement: 452 cubic inches (7.4 liters)

Horsepower: 165

Transmission: 3-speed manual

Wheelbase: 148 inches

Overall Length: 218 inches

Overall Height: 68 inches

Overall Width: 77 inches

There's an intimidation factor of about 9 on a scale of 10 in being perched up behind the bakelite wheel of a V-16 Cadillac Roadster. It's brought on partly by the current value of the car—about 25 grand. On the other hand, with its long tapering hood, the ornament, and the way-up-off-the-ground feeling, the Cadillac is more intimidating than most. It has a Duesenberg air about it—similar styling, hard leather seats, a driving feel that belies its size and era, even the dashboard with all the gauges on a polished insert centered in the middle of a machine-turned, chrome-plated panel. The Fleetwood body is well-proportioned, smoothly executed, and preceded by a radiator of such distinctive size and shape that it could only be a Cadillac. All this confirms Cadillac's overtures to the Duesie market.

But there is one thing missing. When you grind the Duesenberg ever so lightly into first gear and pull away from the curb, you can floor the accelerator and all 6,000 pounds of it start covering a lot of road very quickly. Remember their claim of "88 in second, 116 in top"? Cadillac's gearbox also requires a careful "graunch" into first and an easy bit of clutch/accelerator coordination to get away. There the comparison stops. The engine simply feels anemic. The disappointment comes not in performance per se; it just seems that the car with the first V-16 in our history should have been a real pavement ripper, not a '58 T-Bird.

The Cadillac V-16 needs something besides speed to recommend it as a classic. That something comes from the company's history. The 16-cylinder engine fits properly into the chronology of Cadillac. It's a well-honed, precision piece of machinery and that was founder Henry Leland's forte. Leland & Faulconer Inc. were the leading practitioners of the art of precision manufacturing in 1900. Henry couldn't bear an imperfect grind or a sloppy fit. Likewise he couldn't condone building any piece of machinery without bringing it to its most nearly perfect state. That's basically what got him into the automobile business. A supposedly disastrous fire wiped out the fledgling auto company's factory in March 1901. To get back into production quickly, Ransom E. Olds contracted with the Dodge Brothers and Leland & Faulconer to build engines. From the first wagonload, it was obvious that L & F engines were superior to their Dodge counterparts, but to Leland, it was equally obvious that the engines they were building could be improved. They began to experiment with the huffing one-lunger and by increasing the valve size and open duration, plus improving the timing, they upped horsepower from 3-7/10 to 10-1/4. But Olds rejected the expense of retooling for the more powerful engine. There sat Leland with a better product and no place to sell it.

About that same time, over at the Henry Ford Company, young Henry was getting involved with his second failure. Despite his successful

In Retrospect

1930 Cadillac V16 Roadster   Owner: Harrah's Automobile Collection
Photographed for Motor Trend by John Lamm

racing cars, Ford was still having trouble putting a decent salable street machine together. He failed again and Henry Leland was called in to appraise the machinery of the soon-to-be liquidated company. Leland went to the directors with his appraisal sheet under one arm and an example of the updated Olds engine under the other. He suggested they reorganize the company and build a car with his engine. They agreed, and in August 1902, the company was recapitalized to $300,000 and the name changed to the Cadillac Automobile Company. So Cadillac was formed out of the ashes of the original Ford Motor Company and has lived on to be the oldest auto company to survive in Detroit.

By 1909, Leland had become the head of Cadillac and in that year sold the firm to W.C. Durant, who was forming a new holding company he called General Motors. Leland and son Wilfred stayed on until 1917, then broke with Durant to form the Lincoln Motor Company. The new firm was started to build World War I Liberty aircraft engines and after the Hun was defeated, Leland reformed the company to build cars, introducing the first model in September 1920. It had a 354-cubic-inch V8 developing 81 hp, detachable cylinder heads, and full-pressure lubrication. But the car's looks didn't match its mechanical excellence and Henry Ford achieved some final justice in buying that company from Leland and son in 1922.

The Oldsmobile, Liberty, and Lincoln engines, all refined and respected engines of their day, fit in line with the well-sculptured Cadillac V-16. In fact, Leland had so impressed Durant with his passion for precision that Durant insisted on it in the Cadillac even after the Lelands left GM. Now if you've ever had a chance to scrutinize any pre-1922 automobiles, you know a lot of them were a bit rough—which is understandable to a point in the formative years of the industry. But even in 1910, Cadillac claimed the tolerance on 112 of the pieces in that year's 4-cylinder tourer were accurate to one-thousandth of an inch. The V-16 revived that feeling at Cadillac, being built with the same damn-the-costs attitude that accompanied the designing of the Duesenberg Model J.

The V-16 is actually rather like two overhead-valve straight eights each laid over 22-1/4 degrees from top dead center and bolted to a common aluminum crankcase. With totally separate water pumps, intake and exhaust manifolds, and ignition systems, about the only things the two banks had in common were the five-main-bearing crankshaft and the two-coil (one for each bank) distributor. In fact, the engine was capable of being run one side at a time. Bore and stroke were an even 3 by 4 inches, multiplying out to 452 cubic inches. The horsepower figure for 1930 was 165 at 3,200 rpm, climbing in later years to 180 in 1934, then 185 in 1936. Torque was 320 lbs.-ft. at a loafing 1,500 rpm, which accounts for that easy clutch/accelerator starting procedure. Each bank was fed through a 1-1/4-inch, 1-barrel updraft Cadillac carburetor. The mixture then flowed up and through a four-branch black enameled intake manifold, passed around 1.45-inch intake valves and into cylinders where cast iron pistons compressed it in a ratio of 5.50:1. After firing, the exhaust gases were forced out around 1.45-inch exhaust valves and into a massive shiny exhaust manifold.

But that description doesn't do justice to the Cadillac's quiet, turbine-like response when the combustion process is repeated in sixteen successive cylinders. There is little of the vibration or individual cylinder roar of a four- or even eight-cylinder engine. A brutal step on the accelerator is met with a smooth, sophisticated response that almost rebukes the force that demanded it. The engine is dead quiet compared with others of its era. Some of it is an illusion, the sixteen cylinders in unison producing more of a soothing hum than a bang; some of it is designed-in with hydraulic valve adjusters— forerunners of present-day hydraulic valve lifters. Cadillac added a roller between the cam lobe and lifter and a zero-lash mechanism on the pushrod side of the rocker arm assembly linked by an oil line to an eccentric sleeve on the rocker shaft. As the valves tightened or loosened, the bushing in the eccentric sleeve was rotated hydraulically, raising or lowering the rocker arm and bringing the lash back to zero.

All that smooth, quiet power is transmitted through a ten-inch clutch to Cadillac's own three-speed synchromesh transmission; the same unit bolted up to their standard V-8 power plant. From there it ran back to Cad's rear end, which housed a 4.39:1 ratio. With the average-size V-16 car weighing around 5,500 pounds, this put top speed just over 85 miles per hour, creditable in its day but no match for the Duesenberg it was intended to emulate. Suffering from overweight and high internal engine

The interior featured instruments on a chromed panel in a machine-turned dashboard.

The Cadillac V-16 engine was the first 16-cylinder engine in U.S. automotive history.

friction, fuel consumption was far below par, running in the 6-7 mpg range.

Fleetwood hand-built the coachwork of all the normal V-16's. Roadsters went for $5,350 new. Regardless of the source, even back in the '30s, GM put their money where it showed. The V-16 roadster came at a time when aerodynamic bodies were slipping into vogue, but even though other cars were superior to the Cadillac in speed and handling, few, including some Duesenbergs, looked as good. It started out front with those two Pilot Ray road lamps that swiveled in the direction the car was steered. There is the distinctive grille with the fine wire screen and the five-sided wind wings mounted on both ends of the windshield. Dual spare tires were mounted, one on each side behind the front fender and, like the road wheels, were wires with large spokes. Fine chrome strips ran along the running board pad and decorated the doors of the storage areas (between running board and door on each side), which were expressly designed for a set of golf clubs. In back, a chrome luggage rack folded up neatly behind the body when not in use. From almost any angle, the car looks right. It has that same certain indefinable assembly of lines as the Mercedes SSK or the Locke-bodied KB Lincoln, a personality of design not available in American automobiles now.

Sitting in the cockpit your elbow comes naturally to rest on the top of the door. There is the close-coupled feeling of a cockpit for two, and only two, of the beautiful people going someplace only they could afford to go. The Depression was on, but the old rich still had their money. Eight cylinders was an absolute minimum, twelve was better, and V-16—who would question your credentials?

Frames under the Cadillacs were not the massive steel-girder structures Duesenbergs were built on but were stout for their time, about like your modern one-ton stake truck. Suspension front and rear consisted of straight axles and semi-elliptic springs, 42 x 2-1/4 inches up front, 60 x 2-1/2 inches in back, damped by Lovejoy shocks. As expected, the steering is not in the modern Cadillac class or even the modern truck class, requiring a turning circle of 51 feet compared to 41 feet for the '72 Eldorado. There were 16-1/2-inch mechanical brakes on all four wheels and although they felt hard, they were effective on the car we drove, except for pulling to the left. You wouldn't want to use them many times in succession. Tall 7.50 x 19 tires were used on V-16s, but judging by the various sizes listed for the period, wheel swaps were the great sport of the day.

Cadillac's V-16 was more than just an engineering exercise, of course. The division's

share of the market had slipped under the weight of the Depression. From a sales level of 24,735 cars in 1926, Cadillac was down to 12,078 by 1930, a mere .46 percent of the 2.6 million car market. Cadillac's less expensive LaSalle of 1927 was one wedge against the crumbling sales, the prestigious V-16 (1930) and V-12 (1931) were two more. The 16 stayed on in its overhead valve form until 1937, when it was replaced by another V-16 of flathead design, with 135 degrees between banks. This engine was available until 1940 when, no doubt, the supply finally ran out. We've heard rumors ever since of single overhead cam V-12s hidden under wraps in dark corners of Cadillac engineering, and up until about 18 months ago there seemed some chance of another engine of more than 8 cylinders being marketed by GM. Some stories will hint that the V-12 was dropped because of the anti-smog regulations, others suggest darkly that the engine was just too much a disaster to consider for production. Regardless, we must be content with today's 500-inch engine isolated from us by umpteen pounds of soundproofing and the bean-counter's accounting pads. Somehow, though, I think I'd be happy to give up the air conditioning and stereo radios and cruise control and Kleenex dispensers, taking instead the ancient V-16 roadster, with the engine humming up front where I can hear it . . . just enough.

1929 Miller

1929 MILLER

Engine Type: dual overhead cam in-line 8-cylinder

Displacement: 90 cubic inches (1.5 liters)

Horsepower: 285 (Lockhart engine)

Transmission: 3-speed manual

Wheelbase: 100 inches

Overall Length: 150 inches

Overall Height: 46 inches

Overall Width: 66 inches

"It gets a little light around 110 but I think it would be more stable on a track. We had it up to 5,400 rpm, which would be pretty close to 120, but we just run on the freeway."

The three of us stood across the road looking at the 1921 Miller 91 front drive parked against a weathered fence whose juices had been bleached out years ago by the parching Nevada sun. Together with its sister car of Leon Duray (and a normal rear drive of Tony Gulotta), it had been for years in the Bugatti factory, finally to be reclaimed by the dean of American automotive writers Griff Borgeson, whose personal crusade brought it home.

The car looked completely appropriate in this environment, next to a running fence that could have defined the perimeters of any of a slew of dirt ovals. And yet to the precious few who recall the "golden era of thoroughbred automobile racing," as Griff Borgeson has aptly called it, those converted dirt horse tracks figured little in the Miller epoch. It was the wooden amphitheaters—the "boards"—where the Millers flew.

I wasn't mentally prepared for the machine. It is too small, too pure, too detailed to be a product of the twenties. Leo Duray's car turned one lap of 124.018 mph qualifying at Indianapolis in '28, with a speed unapproached for nine years. The logical outgrowth of cars like this would have been the even smaller, lighter, more aerodynamic vehicles, not the hairy mammoths we had in the forties and fifties. But in the Great Depression, jewel-like race cars faded into a dual limbo of memory and imagination.

You sit low in this car in relation to the cowl, like a modern sprinter, the large, wood-rimmed, four-spoke steering wheel close into your gut. Your left hand falls upon the ball of the outside fuel pressure pump used for start-up until the mechanical, cam-driven pump builds up its head. The fuel pressure gauge is just below and to the left of the 9,000 rpm tach. Water temperature, oil pressure, and supercharger pressure are monitored from an instrument cluster on the right. A tapered, rectangular steel handle on the right operates from the brakes. Its polished knob is a thin-wall aluminum casting.

"It's real hard to see out of it [the Miller]," Smith mentions. "You have to look out either one side or the other. This little deflector really cuts the wind. I drove without this shield and the wind really busts your face. You can just feel the wind pushing your skin in at over a hundred."

Drivers of the period, like Leon Duray and Eddie Miller, Sr., remembered how it was on the boards, how you'd show up for a race and the surface would look good and then deteriorate after a few miles, and how carpenters repaired planks that tore out from underneath while the race was in progress, sticking their heads up through the holes occasionally so that drivers would see human heads seemingly lying on the track. Wood chips and knots littered the track's surface when it began to age and slivers the size

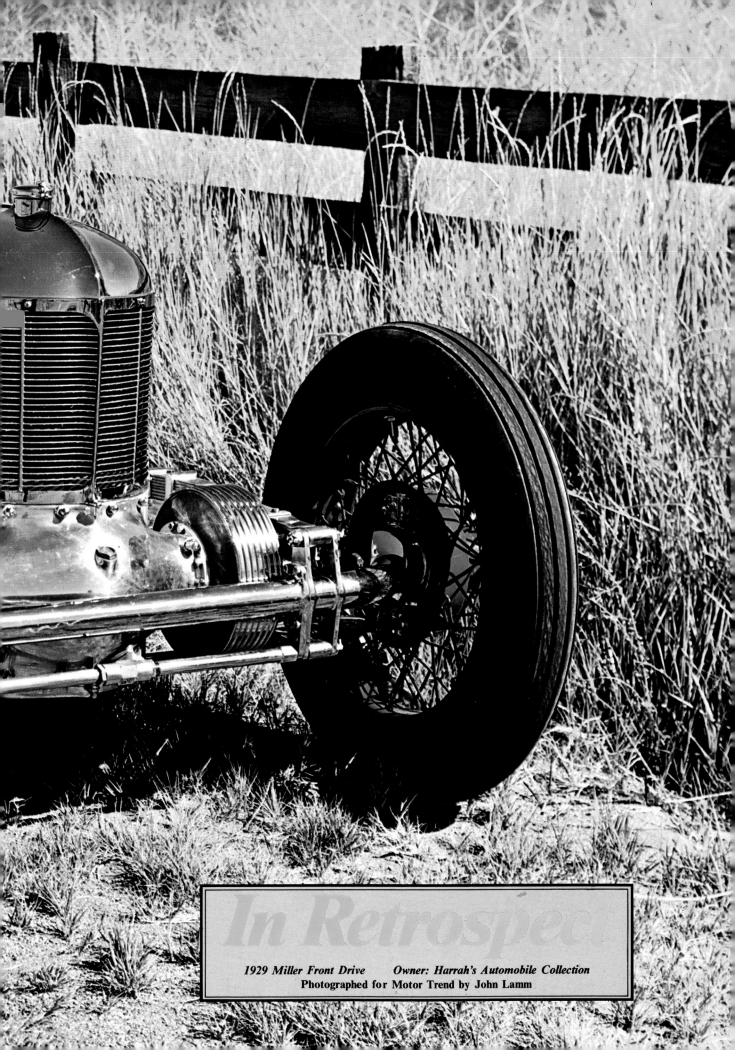

1929 Miller Front Drive   *Owner: Harrah's Automobile Collection*
Photographed for Motor Trend by John Lamm

of fourpenny nails hammered into the driver's skin, then splattered like some dum-dum, hitting a bone. No wonder Duray opted for the paved tracks of Europe.

"The guy [Miller] certainly had taste for engineering a beautiful car," Smith mentions casually. The channel section frames were hand-formed from .125-inch mild steel, sometimes nickel-plated. In the front-drive cars there was only one crossmember, a tube at the back, supplemented by the front-drive mechanism itself and the 25-gallon sheet steel gas tank structure. A 1-1/4-inch diameter steel tube ran through the bottom of the tank, anchoring to the frame channel with a steel ball and brass-socket arrangement. The tank's interior was fully baffled to minimize fuel slosh, tinned to eliminate corrosion and at the back, another ball socket attached to the rear crossmember gave a flexible three-point configuration. Our contemporary, positive-lock, cam and lever fuel cap was a Miller original, circa 1923. You may talk about Colin Chapman's innovative Lotuses using the engine as the rear members but Miller antedated them forty-five years.

"Thunk-chuch, thunk-chuch, thunk-chuch," Smith's muscled left arm begins to put pressure in the fuel tank up to four pounds before the engine is fired off to move the machine down the road a quarter mile. "This has a high-pressure pump that takes over after the engine starts," Smith says as he finishes off the 45-second manual pumping ritual. Only it's not going to be quite that easy. The 2-inch Winfield SR single-throat down-draft carburetor has lost its prime, and cranking over those eight 2.180-inch diameter, 3-ring aluminum pistons and all that associated valve gear with a small handle sticking out the right side of the frame isn't going to make it. So Smith leaps out of the cockpit after we all give it a try and somebody scrounges up an old Coke can and we drain off a little gas from Miller's fuel tank to prime the carburetor. You can see the starting difficulty right away because the fuel must navigate through an 8-inch diameter Miller-designed centrifugal supercharger before it ever gets to the engine's machined, hemispherical, combustion chambers.

Nothing hangs off this engine. That was a Miller trademark from the beginning. Harry Miller was a brilliant machinist-inventor who got involved with racing because he happened to create a carburetor back before World War I

that was unsurpassed at full-throttle. Racing fit his personality because there was always a different challenge, nothing ever congealed to boredom. By 1920, he was building complete race cars, machines that pioneered so many things it's hard to believe they came from a medium-size plant in L.A. Actually the place was a synthesizing factory, for here the best racing technology of the period—Peugeot, Ballot, Duesenberg—was fed into the fertile mind of Miller's gifted designer Leo Goosen, who conjured it into workable reality that in turn was brought to flawless solidity by maybe the best machinist who ever lived, Fred Offenhauser. The full impact of their combined genius can only be evaluated when you consider that the present turbocharged Drakes of the McLarens and the Eagles are really only variations of the smooth Miller theme. Further, their only serious competition in recent times (excluding the turbines), the Ford Indy engine, also derives from much the same design philosophy.

The supercharged 91 Miller came about as a smaller refined version of the successful 122 (121-cubic-inch) straight eight of 1923, which had been in turn a smaller definition of the 183. All of these featured the famous barrel crankcase, which held the crankshaft in a vise-like grip because bronze diaphragms or collars encircled four of the five mains and bolted to the bulkheads. Cylinder blocks were iron, cast in pairs of four cylinders each, with an integral cylinder head. This bolted to the crankcase from the inside using studs and nuts so nothing would interrupt a clean external appearance. Even with twin overhead cams and a full dry-sump oil system the engine weight was 330 pounds, about the same as an aluminum small-block Chevrolet. In its original form with Delco battery ignition and four dual-throat up-draft carburetors, the thing put out 125 hp at 4,000 rpm. Seven years later at half the displacement, the 91 had 285 hp at 8,000 rpm.

The secret, of course, was the supercharging techniques pioneered by Duesenberg and adopted quietly by Miller and refined by Frank Lockhart, who unlocked the secrets of something called an intercooler. With the help of a young Cal Tech engineering student who worked at Miller's, boy wizard Lockhart discovered that the typical superchargers put out heat like a Bessemer converter and if the mixture temperature could be reduced, fantastic power advantages could be realized. At the first

Quarter elliptic springs supported the axle on the Miller front drive.

The finned section of the Miller's engine is a very efficient supercharger intercooler.

race where Lockhart ran it, the car went 8.15 mph faster and established a world's class course record of 144.2.

Parallel to supercharger developments was the order placed at Miller's by Jimmy Murphy for a front-wheel-drive 91. Again Goosen rose to the task by turning the standard Miller 91 engine around 180 degrees and hooking to an ingenious three-speed transmission and differential nested transversely between the front frame rails. By dint of de Dion front suspension, inboard brakes and what amounts to a transaxle, unsprung weight was remarkably low as well as a low profile with a severely dropped rear axle. Engineers in 1926 note at Indianapolis the front drives could lap at almost constant throttle openings, 6,200 rpm on the straight,

6,000 in the turn, as compared to identically powered Millers on formal rear drive that did 7,200 and 5,000 in the same places. At the time, even Detroit, which had often been chagrined by Miller's technological innovation, admitted front-drive had a bright future.

With the introduction of the priming gas, the last running Miller boomed to life in kind of a low moan—a more even, pleasing sound than the turbo-Drakes. Smith climbed into the cockpit and dropped the three-speed transmission into low. The four-plate clutch made from steel buzz saw blades began to take up and the Miller moved off slowly. We kept up for a time in our 351 Montego until the Miller got on cam and faded like a rocket. The last thing we heard was the blower's high-pitched wail.

1939 SS 100 Jaguar

> **1939 SS 100 JAGUAR**
>
> **Engine Type:** overhead valve in-line 6-cylinder
>
> **Displacement:** 2.6 liters (162.5 cubic inches) or 3.5 liters (212.6 cubic inches)
>
> **Horsepower:** 102 (2.6 liter) or 125 (3.5 liter)
>
> **Transmission:** 4-speed manual
>
> **Wheelbase:** 104 inches
>
> **Overall Length:** 150 inches
>
> **Overall Height:** 54 inches
>
> **Overall Width:** 63 inches

It is highly doubtful that Bill (later Sir William) Lyons ever had the faintest clue that his SS cars would someday be collector's items. His *raison d'etre* was making 'em look good and go fast, but cheap. All of his prewar cars were incredibly low-priced, and the SS 100, at about $2,000 for the 2.5-liter version and $2,200 for the 3.5, may have been the most incredible of the lot. It would do all of a hundred in 3.5-liter form, and 0-60 in a shade over ten seconds, and it was gorgeous. One of the English magazines recently referred to the SS 100 as "the cad's car," and it isn't difficult to imagine rotten rogues speeding off into the foggy night, abandoning well-bred former virgins to their weeping mothers.

Bill Lyons started his automotive enterprise as a joint venture with one William Walmsley in Blackpool in 1922. Walmsley had been building sidecars for motorcycles for a couple of years and Lyons was a raving young motorcycle nut who'd just inherited a fair piece of change from his pianomaker father. The firm was called Swallow Sidecar Company, and according to Herb Williamson, writing in *Automobile Quarterly* several years ago, they quickly established themselves as trendsetters in their field. The field was probably not exactly jammed with custom motorcycle sidecar manufacturers, but nonetheless the praise is borne out by the later success of the purely automotive efforts of Lyons and Swallow Sidecar.

The first automotive product was a really slick little custom body for an Austin Seven, introduced in 1926. The Austin Swallow was a great commercial coup, as were virtually all of Lyons' designs, and the firm's automotive future was assured. The little Austins, as bodied by SS, were as right for their time as the Jaguar XK-120 roadsters that Lyons used for his postwar invasion of North America. England was long on car enthusiasm and, with the crash of 1929, short of what today's automotive marketers like to call discretionary income. A truly custom car that set one well apart from the milling throng, without costing much, was mobile manna from Heaven.

Although the SS 100 was a considerably more ambitious effort, it was spawned by exactly the same marketing motivation that was behind that first Austin Swallow. It was descended from a car introduced at the London Motor Show of 1931, the SS 1. The SS 1 was built on a chassis designed specifically by Lyons' people for the purpose, with a Standard "Big Nine" six-cylinder engine and bodywork that knocked the motoring public's collective eye out. SS had been building a Standard Swallow since 1929, but that was just another custom body on an unmodified chassis. The SS 1 was a new car from the ground up, and it marked the end of the old Swallow Sidecar name. By 1932, everything was simply called Swallow, Standard Swallow, or SS, with SS taking over steadily through the thirties. The Standard Swallow marriage lasted twenty years, till 1949, when Lyons' firm, now

called Jaguar Cars, finally abandoned Standard's big old six-cylinder block for one of their own design.

Immediate predecessor of the SS 100 was a transitional model called SS 90, introduced in 1935. It looked very much like the SS 100, but it was powered by a stock Standard side-valve engine. They only built 22 of these, according to the Classic Jaguar Association, and the model was replaced by the 2.5-liter SS 100 in 1936. The SS 100 featured overhead valves in a cylinder head designed by Harry Weslake and cranked out 104 horsepower, for a top speed of about 90. It was the first Jaguar.

The following year saw the coming of the 3.5

Jaguar engine, a bored and stroked version of the 2.5, and a very hot number for its day. It developed 125 bhp and it was quicker by far than anything else at the price. In the four years between '36 and '40, SS built 190 of the 2.5 SS 100 Jaguars and 118 of the 3.5-liter machines. During the same period they continued to manufacture their popular sedan lines, and undoubtedly made a lot of money—something else for which Bill Lyons has always seemed to have a very special talent.

On the day we were to drive the two cars shown here, we were cruising up the Pacific Coast Highway in bright morning sunshine when we suddenly spotted them about a half-

The SS 100 Jaguar engine came in a 2.6-liter version (which delivered about 104 horsepower) and a 3.5 liter version (which developed about 125 horsepower).

mile ahead of us. It was a startling experience, and it's easy to imagine the astonishment of British enthusiasts in the middle thirties when these dreamboats first hit the street. Our two were droning along in formation, in fairly heavy traffic, and they made everything else on the road look like it had been runner-up in a demolition derby. They were small. So red. So shiny. We felt like small boys tearing through the traffic to catch up with them—not just because we had an appointment with their drivers (Holly Hollenbeck and George Sirus), but because we were dying for a closer look. I

had driven SS 100s before, had practically owned one as a matter of fact, but here I was all out of breath, behaving like I'd never seen one.

For some reason, Mr. Hollenbeck's 2.5 was more fun to drive than Mr. Sirus' 3.5. The 2.5-liter car seemed lighter and quicker—although there's really no difference in weight—and the brakes worked better. Both cars had mechanical brakes, as did all Jaguars up to 1949, and evidently the extremely critical business of proper adjustment was more carefully attended to on the smaller-engined car. On the purely emotional side, Mr. Hollenbeck's car also had a

leaping Jaguar mascot mounted on the radiator cap, and this added some spice to the driving.

Like all cars of the period, the SS 100 does not lend itself to the now-classic Farina straight-arm driving position. Evidently the hairy-armed heroes of the thirties liked hurtling along with elbows pointed due east and due west, which must have been a trial when the side curtains were in place. The steering wheel is adjustable, as is the driver's seat, but only between "too close" and "much too close." No other alternatives are available.

Gear shifting requires good hand-and-foot coordination and a well-tuned ear. The engine—in either size—feels like it's expending most of its energy just to make a gargantuan flywheel revolve, and this tends to discourage deft little jabs at the throttle for rev-adjustment-while-endeavoring-to-shift-the-old-brute. Like all sixes, the engine is dead-smooth, with a lovely baritone drone that lulls one into a blissful feeling of splendid automotive isolation. There is you, and there is this car (with this smoothly droning six-banger at work up front), and

everything is quite obviously going to be all right. This is especially true when you're operating it with the windscreen folded down. This eliminates turbulence, directs all the wind straight past your ears instead of up the back of your neck, and further isolates you from the mundane concerns of modern corporate man by making conversation impossible.

It is 1939 again, you look like Leslie Howard, you have your pick of the best women in London, and your worst problem is that the bloody Germans may have the poor taste to muck up your planned motor trip to the Balkans. Your flaming red SS 100 responds to your every command as any faithful steed should. Ask a man in such a state to imagine a tenth of the concerns that probably confront you as you herd your Mercury Marquis down Main Street this morning, and he'd reckon you were losing your mind. And you probably are. Listen. Take the money you were going to spend on your shrink, or marriage counselor, or whatever, and buy yourself an SS 100. You'll feel better.

1955 Ford Thunderbird

1955 FORD THUNDERBIRD

Engine Type: overhead valve V-8

Displacement: 292 cubic inches (4.7 liters)

Horsepower: 198

Transmission: 2-speed automatic

Wheelbase: 102 inches

Overall Length: 175.3 inches

Overall Height: 51.9 inches

Overall Width: 70.3 inches

The Thunderbird, if you were to believe a 1954 Ford Motor Company press release, was a "mythical bird supposed to cause thunder, lightning, and rain," and symbolizing "power, swiftness, and prosperity." Precisely the attributes an American ripening in affluence wanted to hear about.

Those GIs who had come home a decade before were now firmly established in the booming economy spotted with new fields like computers and aerospace and were rewarding themselves with toys like sports cars and hi-fis.

Neither the Thunderbird nor the Corvette was the first postwar home-grown two-seater on the market; the Pinin-Farina-bodied Nash-Healey, Kaiser-Darrin, and a number of other low production cars had preceded them. But the two-seat Thunderbird remains one of the more significant cars of the post-Korea, pre-Vietnam Golden Age, because of what it was and what it wasn't.

It wasn't a sports car. Even Ford knew that. Although Thunderbird ads claimed "breath-taking, trigger-torque acceleration," they didn't talk too much about cornering. And no wonder.

The 102-inch wheelbase and nose-heavy 3,300-odd-pound curb weight didn't exactly make four-wheel drifts a plannable maneuver.

The two-seat 'Bird was obviously aimed at a luxury-oriented market, the kind of guys who wore Ben Hogan caps and baggy Perry Como cashmere sweaters. Accordingly, the list of options was a long one—automatic transmission; power steering; brakes and windows; four-way power seat; fender skirts and various glittery chrome bagatelles for the exterior, wheels, and engine. It also had a telescoping steering column, presumably to accommodate growth in the driver's girth.

Although the Thunderbird followed the Corvette by two years, that first 1955 model scooped the '55 Corvette in a couple of ways. First, it had roll-up windows instead of the clumsy side curtains of the early 'Vettes. Secondly, it started right out with a V8, instead of first offering six-cylinder engines. In '55, Chevy debuted their great 265 and made it available as an extra-cost option in the Corvette, but the T-Bird's 295 V8 was standard.

The short-stroke Y-block 295-cubic-inch V8 had been introduced the year before, and Chevy grudgingly admitted in private that it had measurably better longevity than their glorious 265. The Ford engine was rated at 193 horses with a 3-speed stick or 198 horses with the automatic tranny, the difference due to a higher 8.5:1 compression ratio (obtained by use of thinner head gaskets). Dual exhausts were standard, exhaling through the rear bumper guards, and all the 'Birds enjoyed a four-barrel carb.

The mid-50s were a no-holds-barred era in the American auto industry and for every move that Chevy made in racing, Ford was quick to react. When Chevy jumped from a 265-inch V8 in '55 to

In Retrospect

1955 Ford Thunderbird   Owner: Maybelle Barr
Photographed for Motor Trend by John Lamm

a 283 in '57, Ford retaliated by adding two 312 cu. in. V8s to the Thunderbird option list. Actually all-out war was declared with Ford offering four engines for the T-Bird, the hottest being a 285-hp dual four-barrel job. There were even a few 300-hp Paxton-McCulloch supercharged jobs built, to counter those super-hot fuel-injected Corvettes from Messrs. Ed Cole and Zora Duntov.

The styling of the '55 Thunderbird was wonderfully simple. In an attempt to save money, many parts, such as headlight rims and taillights, were borrowed from the larger Ford sedans but, basically, the 2-seater 'Bird had a functionality of line unmatched by any American car since.

Among collectors, the most prized of any particular car model is always the very first or the very last of the series. Thus, the '55 and '57 Thunderbirds are likely to be higher-priced than the '56s. Today, a clean, original-condition Thunderbird goes for close to its original price—

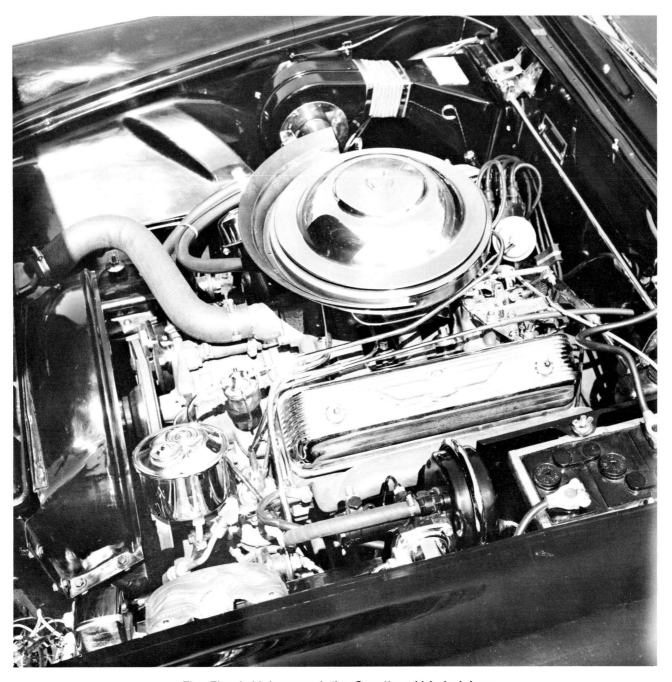

The Thunderbird scooped the Corvette, which had been introduced two years earlier, by making the 295 V-8 engine standard equipment.

$3,296 with hardtop standard and clothtop an option extra—while a mint "concours" one can bring $5,000.

Driving the two-seat 'Bird is a trip back to the mid-50s. Start it up and the dual exhausts have that "Hollywood muffler" rasp. It won't corner vigorously, and it won't stop many times from 60 mph. In fact, axle tramp both during acceleration and braking is enough to make traction bars a necessity, according to some owners. But the power steering is easy. The car is woman-sized, which may account for the fact that you see mostly women driving them.

The car shown here—one of the first twelve off the line—is the result of two years of diligent effort by Mr. and Mrs. Darrell Barr, of Beverly

The wheels of Maybelle Barr's 'Bird are Kelsey-Hayes knock-offs with more chrome than Ford originally intended Thunderbird wheels to have.

Hills. Mrs. Barr has owned four different two-seat 'Birds, but finally decided that she would concentrate on restoring a '55 and a '57. She found a '55 in California (where 40% of the 2-seaters were sold) that had no rust and all the options. She bought it in 1971 for $1,100 and has since spent over $5,000 restoring it to original condition.

To say Maybelle Barr is a perfectionist may not be going far enough. She had the upholstery redone, was not satisfied, and had it done all over again. The entire suspension was replaced with new parts. The bolts on the chassis have been upgraded to rust-proof stainless steel hardware. Maybelle does admit to overdoing her 'Bird for visual effect. To wit: the chrome wire wheels are real Kelsey-Hayes knock-offs from a '63 with more chrome than Ford originally applied. But Maybelle will change to the stock wheels or spray black paint over the chrome if the concours judge insists on being a super-purist.

The Barr 'Bird is so perfect that it stole a Best of Show trophy from a gaggle of Rolls and Duesies at a recent concours.

In 1958, Ford introduced the four-seater Thunderbird, a car which, most collectors agree, has no value whatsoever. It looked rather like a jukebox in the prone position, with tires under it. Certainly it bears no relation other than name to its original kin. Ford's concept turnabout was one of the great losses to the American enthusiast. Who knows where evolution would have led. Maybe Mercury's present two-seater, the Italian-built $10,000 Pantera, is what the two-seat Thunderbird could have become.

Be that as it may, with the introduction of the four-seater, Ford inadvertently elevated the two-seater T-Bird to semi-"classic" status and, even though concours d'Elegance judges used to look askance at postwar cars, you'll find a few mint two-seat 'Birds taking away the gold.

I saw a '55 on Sunset Boulevard the other day. It was black, with the top down and a tonneau cover trimly snapped over the passenger area. The driver was about fifty, wearing sunglasses, a cableknit turtleneck sweater and bare-knuckled driving gloves. He was tooling along, the wind wafting what grey hair stuck out from under his PoorBoy golf cap. There was still something grand about this guy and his two-seat T-Bird roadster, something indefinably grand and typically American—that we lost along the way.

BMW 507

BMW 507

Engine Type: overhead valve V-8

Displacement: 3.1 liters (193 cubic inches)

Horsepower: 160

Transmission: 4-speed manual

Wheelbase: 97.5 inches

Overall Length: 172.6 inches

Overall Height: 49.5 inches

Overall Width: 65 inches

Gunther Kiehl works for BMW—Bayerische Motoren Werke, or Bavarian Motor Works—and his job is to do for BMW what he did at Mercedes-Benz, create a corporate museum. I went to see him to talk about the BMW 507. BMW can trace its history from a World War I aircraft engine builder through big, hairy motorcycles and oddball minicars to manufacturers of some of the finest automobiles that ever set the autobahn on fire. Somewhere in there—around the time of the motorcycles and minicars—came the 507, a car totally out of its time (a decade too soon . . . or too late), a car that today, with fifteen years on the odometer and running on hard rubber, can still keep a BMW 2002tii at bay. And nobody ever called a 2002tii slow.

Zero to sixty? About seven seconds flat. Top speed? Between 128 and 138 mph, depending on axle ratio. The 507 could cover a full mile—from a standing start—in less than 42 seconds, coming out the far end at better than 117 mph. The 507 was—and is—a fast car.

The BMW isn't perfect, however. It has performance, but the suspension is not really up to it in all conditions. With its torsion bar springing, equal length upper and lower control arms in front and live axle at back, the ride is firm, without a lot of articulation. You find pretty quickly the car dances across rough pavement. On the autobahnen, however, and normally smooth secondary roads, the 507 presses forward at a long-legged rhythm, if not with the turbine smoothness of BMW's current sports coupe then certainly like a Camaro Z/28.

BMW's whole 507 adventure began in November 1954 when Max Hoffman, the most notable and outspoken of their several U.S. distributors, was shown a prototype sports car by chief engineer Fritz Fiedler at the Bauer coachworks in Stuttgart. Built on the massive BMW 502 sedan chassis and powered by something Americans understood, a V-8, Fiedler felt the car fit the American market perfectly.

What you have to understand is that nobody was building V-8s in Germany in the Fifties. Nobody but BMW. The standard European engine of that era was a one-and-a-half liter four-cylinder. Extremes ranged from about 1100cc to maybe two liters. So what's BMW doing? Building a 600cc minicar and a 3.2-liter V-8. (It was to be 1963 before BMW straightened out and started to fly right with its enormously successful range of 1.6-, 1.8-, and 2.0-liter sedans.)

Recalling that Chevrolet and then Ford had just embarked on similar projects, Fiedler's long-range vision seems remarkable. The rugged 502 box-section frame and 507 body structure would be welded together into one rigid unit with an aluminum outer skin, doors, and fenders. Hoffman had previously imported some thirty 502 sedans into the U.S. and was familiar with their good power and performance, but the prototype's styling put him off and he began searching for a designer to execute his ideas. In the end this turned out to be

Albrecht Goertz, who had just terminated an association with Raymond Loewy and work that included designing Studebaker's postwar cars, especially the spectacular Starlite coupe.

After one false start that looked too much like a revised T-Bird for Hoffman, the final 507 drawings were approved and sent to BMW in Munich. All through these negotiations, Hoffman had steadfastly insisted on a selling price under $5,000, a stipulation that augured an initial production order to 5,000 units. Hoffman admitted years later he never felt the factory had anything like the capacity to manufacture the 507 in such quantities, a judgment proved correct by history.

Introduced at the Frankfurt Auto Show in September 1955, the very un-Teutonic 507, with its sweeping, sexy lines, was an immediate hit. By early 1957, the car was announced in New York at just under five grand, but an extremely low volume quickly raised the sticker to eight thousand dollars, where it remained throughout the model's entire four-year production run of 263 cars.

Big, powerful, simple overhead-valve engine. Racy styling and front engine/rear drive, with adequate but not superior suspension. It all sounds so American. Maybe the 507 is best understood as sort of a German two-seater Thunderbird (detailed in a way no T-Bird could ever be), a sports-personal car exclusively for the wealthy American car nut who abhorred the idea of buying a machine from a Ford or Chevy dealer.

You sit low in a 507, legs stretched forward from the deep bucket seat to the pendulum clutch and brake pedals. Anyone over six feet is going to be cramped in this car, although it looks as if the seat tracks could be fiddled with for more travel. Directly ahead of the driver, through the Porsche-like four-spoke steering wheel, is an instrument nacelle much like the ones facing you in present BMWs, Mercedes, and Audis. A large 160-mph speedometer on the

left and 6,000-rpm tach on the right blank an electric clock. The bottom part of the speedometer is given over to high beam indicator, oil light, oil pressure gauge, turn signal light, and ignition light, while temperature and gasoline gauges lie under the tachometer. All the driver's controls are well placed and easy to manipulate.

As soon as you let out the 507's very light hydraulic clutch you know this is one of those rare timeless machines you want to live with forever. The engine's 197 lbs.-ft. of torque is generated at around 4,000 rpm, but this is not one of those peaky power plants you have to trick into forward motion. As you move off, there is just this powerful throb from the throaty dual exhausts as the car gathers speed. A light touch pulls the short, delicate shift lever into second gear. Like the rest of the vehicle, the four-speed transmission is as cultivated as a Bavarian shooting piece.

A decade and a half ago, not a lot of thought was given to things like flow-through ventilation, and yet here are individual, adjustable fresh air vents for either side, with a two-speed fan assist. Interestingly, 507 ventilation is more effective than the system BMW has in their current model range.

The 507's pinion-and-segment steering is quick and light—too light for the good road feel an automobile like this demands. For all its lightness, a lot of road shock ricochets back through the steering wheel on uneven surfaces and fast curves. And yet, with nearly 50/50% weight distribution, the 507 has a hint of the speed feel later BMWs would become famous for.

We spent the better part of a day driving around lower Bavaria with Gunther Kiehl and his 507 and trying to decide whether America would have loved the car in 1957 if they'd been given the chance. When we were done, we learned that this very car had been put at Pvt. Elvis Presley's disposal while he served his time in Germany. When he came home, the BMW stayed behind.

1947 MG TC

1947 MG TC

Engine Type: overhead valve in-line 4-cylinder

Displacement: 1.2 liters (76.2 cubic inches)

Horsepower: 54

Transmission: 4-speed manual

Wheelbase: 94 inches

Overall Length: 144.5 inches

Overall Height: 53.2 inches

Overall Width: 56 inches

Almost everybody who has had anything to do with cars has been involved at some time or another with early MGs. Each knows of someone who is presently in the restoration process, another who used to have an MG "back before I was married," and even a few who own one now. But why? The MG TCs that materialized in small, hidden showrooms after World War II weren't much by today's standards. They were slow, rock hard riding, with only moderately good handling, impossible repairability, and bad brakes. But they were all we had, and they nailed themselves firmly in the Walter Mitty corners of 1948 minds.

At 70 miles per hour, with the windscreen folded flat, the breeze flowing in over that long TC hood made your eyes water, then trailed the tears back across your ears. Your hair got whipped and if you drove long enough and hard enough, your face glowed pink with windburn. The car would top out at only 75 miles per hour, but that close to the ground, with the door sloping down at the back, it felt like 90. So what if it didn't handle that well, it cornered vastly

better than Detroit's offerings and at least the shorter wheelbase and the quick Bishop cam steering made it feel right.

Hard ride was a problem for a lot of owners, until they joined the "required" sports car club and were instilled with the creed: "If it ain't snowing or raining too hard to see, you leave the top down." That spirit pervaded the entire sense of the owner and bolstered his behind against the coal-cart suspension. Besides, with all that wind, rain, sun, and dust, his body was too numb to notice the ride most of the time. In the same myopic spirit, he didn't worry about the weak brakes, because the really neat thing was to use the gearbox for slowing the car. The 5.12:1 final drive ratio helped.

As for repairs, let's just say that there are a lot of men on both coasts living in beautiful homes and driving rather expensive cars on the surplus profits they accumulated in the '40s and '50s fixing MGs. It was a matter of ill-suited supply and dewy-eyed demand. The wealth would not have come as easily if the MGs had been finicky, high-strung cars, but happily, they weren't. Problems of repair were, in the main, confined to getting the parts.

Left over from prewar Great Britain, the MG TC is basically a 1939 MG TA with synchromesh on the top three gears. Foundation for the TC is a simple ladder frame, covered with a steel and oak body. What passes for the suspension is somewhat the same front and rear. There are iron axles, beam in front, live in rear, clamped to unyielding leaf springs. Dampening is by Girling lever shocks. The suspension is so stiff that much of the road compliance is supplied by frame flex. The rudimentary brakes are little iron drums, 9 inches in diameter by 1.5 inches wide. The wheels to which they are attached through knock-off hubs are the spidery 19 by 2.5-inch wire hoops mounting 4.50 x 19 Dunlops,

In Retrospect

1947 MG-TC Owner: Mike Goodman
Photographed for Motor Trend by John Lamm

which gave rise to the description of a sports car as a "coffin riding on four harps."

Power for the TC is also basic—a simple, overhead valve, long-stroke four-banger of 76.3 cubic inches. Pressure is a low, 54.4 bhp at 5,200 rpm, torque 64 lbs.-ft. at 2,700. While the engine's demands include the "don't let the revs run below 2,000" rule, it stood up fairly well to the uninitiated American driver who was used, in 1947, to dropping his Ford into third at 20 mph. Carburetion is by two SUs that ration premium fuel at the rate of one gallon every 22 miles. Bolted on behind that small engine is a four-speed transmission with synchromesh on the top three gears, the interesting point being that the TC's modern counterpart, the 1,300cc MG Midget, still has synchro only on the top three gears. First is still a graunch.

The interior is as straightforward as the rest of the car. Hide-covered seats have individual and adjustable cushions, but share a common back that is also adjustable. Although the steering wheel has both reach and rake adjustments, the only people able to affect the classic arms-out driving position are those too short to reach the pedals. Directly in front of the driver is a large chronometric (which means it staggers) tachometer enclosing a small clock. The speedometer (with odometer and trip mileage readouts) is at the passenger side of the panel, probably on the premise that an MG TC would never attain a velocity sufficient to frighten anyone but the driver; all the other instruments and controls live in symmetrical splendor between the two big dials: There's a real ammeter, genuine oil pressure indicator, a horn button you can press without removing your hand from the wheel rim, ditto for the headlight dimmer, a combination sidelight-headlamp-ignition switch, starter pull (that's right—pull), mixture pull, foglamp switch, 12-volt taps, ignition warning light, panel light switch, a dynamite slow-running (we call it "throttle") control, and over in front of the pilot a fuel warning light that tends to ignite itself according to a set of whims not readily comprehended but seldom associated with the quantity of fuel on board. Separately controlled map lights for driver and passenger wrap it up. Crowning the whole business is one of the world's least useful rear-view mirrors.

Original TC tops were fairly tight waxed sailcloth and quite easy to operate. There are no glass windows, proper clear plastic side curtains

Viewing the MG TC from the rear, one can see the gas tank, hidden between the spare wheel and the body, and the full complement of instruments on the dash.

assuming that function. All buttoned up, the car is—in a word—snug.

The sports car movement didn't get started in this country with roll-up windows, hydraulic tops, big engines, and .85g lateral accelerations. It started with the $1,895 TC. As did such racing luminaries as Richie Ginther, Phil Hill, and the late, great Kin Miles.

Lord Nuffield's next model, the 1950 TD, got the independent front suspension and two models later, the 1955 TF got a larger but short-lived 1500cc engine. Aerodynamics were discovered with the introduction of the MGA in 1956 and updated in the MGB in 1962. Sadly, the next letter car, the MGC, was a miscegenation of MGB body and 6-cylinder Austin-Healey engine. After a short period of embarrassment, the MGC was removed from the market. As the price of the senior MG grew toward its present $3,200, the MG Midget, a slicked-up version of the now-lamented Austin-Healey Sprite, was

added to the line. But even with front disc brakes, quicker acceleration, and superior handling, the Midget is not as desirable as the TC, even if the 1947 car were sold at the same price, instead of the $3,000-odd you must pay for a good one today.

Why? Because, at 70 miles per hour, with the windscreen folded flat, the breeze flowed in over that long TC hood, made your eyes water, then trailed the tears back across your ears. Your hair got whipped and. . . .

1941 Lincoln Continental

1941 LINCOLN CONTINENTAL

Engine Type: L-head V-12

Displacement: 292 cubic inches (4.7 liters)

Horsepower: 120

Transmission: 3-speed manual

Wheelbase: 125 inches

Overall Length: 209.8 inches

Overall Height: 62 inches

Overall Width: 73.3 inches

Even today, the '41 Lincoln Continental is a lot of car. Take the styling, for example. It's still the "now" look thirty years after Edsel Ford and Eugene Gregorie brought it to this country and modernized it. A clean '40 or '41 Continental still stops people cold on the street. Thirty years ago performance was a strong point of the Continental and even today they don't have to take any sass from half of the cars on the road if they're in any kind of decent shape. And handling? Compared to the other prestige cars of that era they were practically sports cars, about the only things on this side of the Atlantic that could outhandle them being the smaller products of the Ford line. The cross-sprung, solid axle suspension shared by Fords, Mercurys, Zephyrs, and Continentals alike was considered a fairly high state of the art for the period, even being used in more refined form on Indy and sprint racers both post- and pre-World War II. Even today, if one isn't afraid to utilize drift, a Continental will give a number of modern cars a tough act to follow on a relatively smooth but twisting road.

The car that was to set a styling trend lasting for over thirty years had its beginning in 1938. Edsel Ford, as President of the Ford Motor Co., had long been interested in what he referred to as "Continental" styling. In fact, he and Gregorie, during the thirties, had designed and run up a number of cars on Ford chassis with long hoods and front fenders and other European design features. But in every case Edsel's wishes to produce cars that combined custom flavor and mass production were thwarted by old-line Ford production men, and the cars never got beyond the one-off stage.

One day in 1938 Edsel suggested that Gregorie design a special car for Ford's own use. It was to be based on the Lincoln Zephyr, and Ford handed the designer a number of sketches of the car he wanted. A tenth-sized clay model was mocked up. Meeting with Edsel's approval, the model was turned over for a full engineering prototype with Edsel following every move. Using Zephyr panels, the prototype staff sliced four inches out of the vertical height and added twelve inches to the hood and front fenders. During this period, Edsel was pleased enough with the results to order another pair for his sons Benson and Henry II. So actually there were three prototypes, not one.

Satisfied that the work was underway as he wanted, Edsel took off for a vacation in Florida. He left orders that the first one finished was to be shipped to him there, and so, in March, 1939, the first Continental to see the light of day, eagle gray with gray leather upholstery, arrived. It was an immediate sensation, so much so that Edsel came home to Dearborn with 200-odd requests for copies. This plus the interest generated by the other two cars finally got through to the old-liners and the decision was made to produce a limited batch of 500. Tooling was begun in October of '39 and the first 25 cars

In Retrospect

1941 Lincoln Continental Cabriolet Owner: Lloyd P. Whitworth
Photography: John Lamm

were completed in December, all convertibles. A hard-top coupe version was designed, and from then on all the following cars of the batch were designated as 1940 models. From October 1939 to September 1940 a total of 394 cars were built, 350 coupes and a mere 44 Cabriolets.

Engines for these cars were ordinary 1940 Zephyr V12s, but they were given polished alloy heads and intake manifolds set off by chrome acorn nuts. Compression ratio was 7.2 to 1, bore was 2.875 in. and stroke was 3.75 for a total of 292 cubic inches. Rated horsepower was 120 at

When ordinary Zephyr V-12 engines were used in the Continental, they were given polished alloy heads and intake manifolds set off by chrome acorn nuts.

3,600 rpm and torque was given as 225 lb.-ft. at 1,800 rpm. It doesn't sound like much but it should be remembered that anything over 100 bhp at that time was considered to be more than adequate. Coupled with the smoothness produced by twelve cylinders and a lot of piston area, it felt like more than 120 horses lived under that hood.

With 1941 came refinements. The most obvious of these were the pushbutton door releases that replaced the door handles on the '40 models. Another was a slight change in the grille inserts, the vertical bars being surrounded by a rim rather than being left open at the ends. The Lincoln-Zephyr insignia was dropped from hubcaps and horn button and a tasteful script

Lincoln Continental in metal was appliqued on the cowl and spare tire cap. Not so obvious were springs that were longer by two inches in the front and two-and-a-half inches at the rear, each leaf being separated by rubber inserts. The sixteen-inch wheels were widened to five inches from 4-1/2 and shod with 7.00 x 16 rubber. Directional signals became standard equipment and the radio could be controlled by a foot switch that changed stations at full tromp and shut down commercials at half-pedal. More important was an automatic overdrive that was optional in place of the two-speed Columbia rear axle that graced the '40 versions.

After 1941 the Continental went downhill. The 1942 model year, beginning in October, was notable for a number of things, mostly catastrophic. First, someone who had apparently been impressed with the Burlington Zephyr got the upper hand in styling the Continental fenders and hood with the inevitable result that the car looked as though it had been driven under a Ford truck, emerging with the truck's fenders and front end. Then, some aggressive people from across the Pacific made a mess out of Pearl Harbor, which stopped production on all cars for the four war years.

In 1946, production of cars for civilians, including a new version of the Continental, was resumed. This time the stylist in charge had been impressed by a Cadillac. A heavy, waffle-iron grille and an equally heavy bumper were plastered on the front. On the sides the graceful flowing fenders had given way to a set of boxy pieces of sheet metal that looked as if, like the grille, they had been subcontracted to that section of the Fisher plant that supplied Cadillac. In addition, the postwar price spiral pushed the cost from the $2,800 price of the '41 to $5,000 for the '46. Lacking the sheer class of the '40 and '41, hung with the 60 percent price increase and faced into the bargain with a Cadillac campaign to become THE prestige car on the American market, the Continental was doomed.

At the end of 1948 the Continental program was quietly dropped; the Lincoln Continental was gone.

1931 Duesenberg Model J

1931 DUESENBERG MODEL J

Engine Type: dual overhead cam in-line 8-cylinder

Displacement: 420 cubic inches (6.8 liters)

Horsepower: 265

Transmission: 3-speed manual

Wheelbase: 154 inches

Overall Length: 221 inches

Overall Height: 67 inches

Overall Width: 75 inches

It's tempting to write about Duesenbergs in a style reminiscent of *The Guinness Book of World Records*. There certainly is plenty of material. Land speed records in 1920; Indy victories in '24, '25, and '27; Ab Jenkins's '35 one-hour record at Bonneville; the Mormon Meteor III; and the 1921 victory in the International Grand Prix at Le Mans with Jimmy Murphy. But those speeds and dates are of thirty years ago, many broken, the rest forgotten. What remains of the Duesenbergs has little to do with numbers.

It has a lot to do with the car itself. Behind the eighteen-inch steering wheel of the 1931 Model J Tourster, way up off the ground, you feel less a driver than a captain, hustling this huge car around abandoned streets in Thousand Oaks, California, working, but enjoying it. The engine hums with a ticking whirr as the valves ride up and down the spinning lobes of dual overhead cams. It is loafing at 500 rpm idle. When you ease the gearbox back into first and slowly move all 5,700 pounds away from the curb, don't expect to feel truck-like handling or response. And don't expect to chug slowly along, because even though this is a 1931 Duesenberg, its

engine was rated at 265 horsepower and that goes all the way up to 4,200 rpm. "88 in second, 116 in top," the ads claimed, and I've only heard one person dispute that.

You can wait and shift at 4,000 or go ahead and pop it into third at thirty miles per hour—the engine doesn't seem to care. If it did, you'd know right away, from one of the myriad instruments on the shiny engine-turned dash. You have the speedometer and tach and all the rudimentary gauges you expect in any complete auto, but some of the dials look unfamiliar. There's an altimeter-barometer on the right, and just above the speedo is a brake pressure gauge. At each end of the dash are reminder lights, run off a gear-crammed timing box next to the fuel pump, that shine to help you remember car maintenance. One glows red to tell you that a little plunger is driving oil out to chassis lube points like the spring shackles and shock connections, while the green one next to it lets you know there's oil in the reservoir. Another light tells you that 700 miles have gone by since your last oil change, yet another blinks bright every 1,400 miles to remind you that the battery needs water.

Inspired by Gordon Buehrig, the body was executed by Durham and first built on the long, 153-1/2-inch wheelbase chassis for the 1931 New York Auto Salon. It was called the Tourster, but after Gary Cooper bought the first one, it was unofficially named after him. Even Cooper, who looked so tall on the screen going after the scruffy bad guys in *High Noon*, seemed a midget in that huge car. Done in aluminum, it starts at the front with the familiar Duesenberg grille, flanked by a pair of those big headlamps, then back over the hood (which makes up almost half the car's entire length and has those graceful louvers radiating forward from the

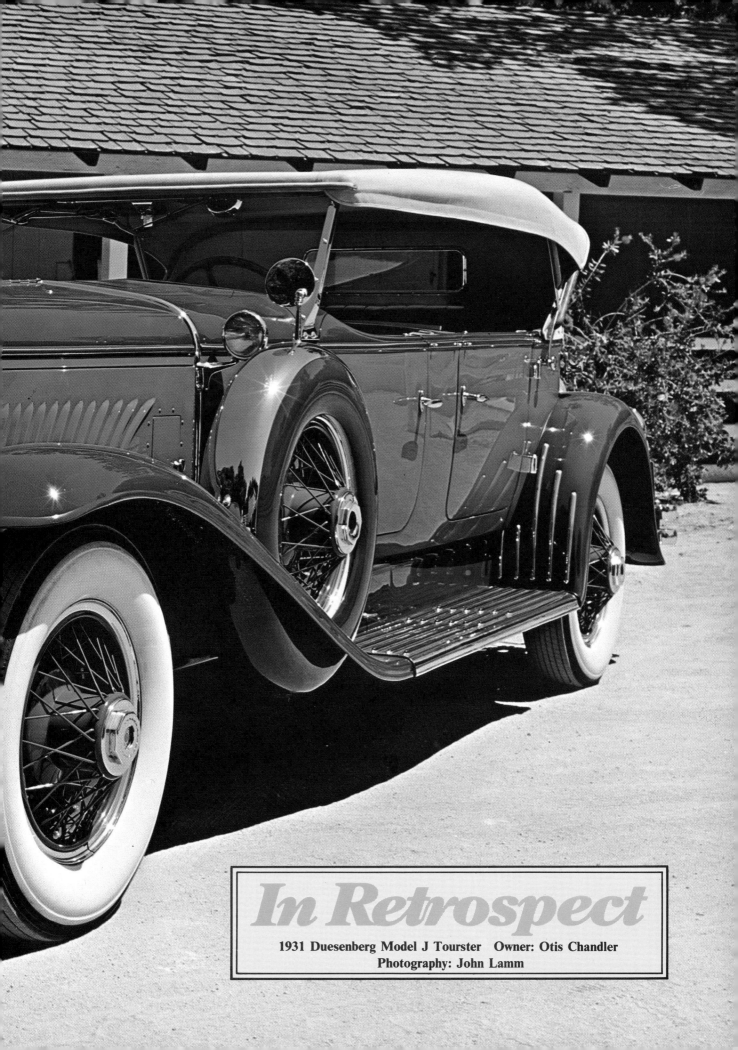

In Retrospect

1931 Duesenberg Model J Tourster   Owner: Otis Chandler
Photography: John Lamm

spare wheels). Front and rear passenger compartments are separated by a small cowl that contains a wind-up window. The interior is protected by a top done in Burbank canvas, the same material that covers the multi-compartment trunk hiding behind the body.

Fred Duesenberg figured that most of the wobble and shimmy in cars of that era came from excessive frame flex, so he based his cars on a 7/32″ alloy steel frame that had rails some 8-1/2 inches high. With five heavy crossmembers, no Duesenberg wobbled or shimmied. It wouldn't dare. There are semi-elliptic springs front and rear, an I-beam front axle and huge solid axle in back with 2-3/16-inch axle shafts bored out for lightness. A torque tube stretches from the heaviest crossmember up front to the rear end to keep the rear springs from winding up when that dohc eight gets to churning out all 265 horsepower.

Engines were Fred Duesenberg's forte and the straight eight in the Model J put a lot of his best together. E.L. Cord, who had bought Duesen-

The dashboard not only has all the instrument gauges you would expect, but some you wouldn't, including several maintenance reminder lights.

berg and Lycoming to add to the Auburn Motor Co. sent men into Duesenberg's Indianapolis factory to take over the menial administration and let Fred and his brother Augie get into the no-money-spared Model J program. The 420-cubic-inch eight came out a year and a half later,

The Duesenberg engine was rated at 265 horsepower and has special design features to damp out engine vibration and insure a smooth ride.

two cams ticking away and four valves per cylinder working in unison with aluminum rods and pistons traveling 4-3/4 inches up and down the 3-3/4-inch bores.

The thoroughness and thought in the design are demonstrated in particular by the system installed to damp out vibrations. Like any long in-line engine, the Duesenberg eight suffered from harmonic vibrations at certain rpm. To damp out the vibrations, sealed cartridges 94 percent full of mercury were bolted to opposite sides of the crank cheek between cylinders 1 and 2. When the crank went into a vibration period, it twisted first one way, then the other, forcing the mercury back and forth over two baffles in the cartridge. Friction between the mercury and baffles and within the mercury itself snuffed out the vibration so it was unnoticeable.

Interesting as the car may have been underneath, what counted was the status, the same ego-puffing thrill that sends people into Cadillac, Lincoln, and Mercedes showrooms now. The Duesenbergs were designed to appeal to established wealth. In one ad, for instance, a white-haired master-of-his-fate, stands calm on the deck of a yacht, obviously HIS yacht, a pipe held loosely in his lips, the tie flapping out of his V-neck sweater. Binoculars hang from his neck and behind him a properly outfitted sailor grips a huge wheel. Below, in very 1930ish script type

is the one line, "He drives a Duesenberg." That ad appeared in the May 1934 issue of *Vanity Fair* and was followed by others that just showed one car, a bit of filigree, the name of the body style, and the line, "The World's Finest Motor Car." Nothing loud or gaudy, but just enough.

When Duesenberg began delivering the Model J in 1929, they delivered a bit more than just a long, beautiful body, a powerful engine, and status. They sent along a good measure of pride. For the first time since the war, Americans had a car, or at least a chassis, they could put up against the Europeans. There was no need to take a second to the Bentley, Mercedes, Hispano-Suiza or even the Bugatti. Here was an American car that kings and maharajahs could buy (several did, and one car eventually ended up in Siberia complete with hot plate and toilet).

It all ended in August of '37. The greatest of what Bill Mitchell, vice president of styling at GM calls, "those long-hooded babes" went with the sale of Cord Corporation. The buildings were sold that October and all that was left were parts and repeated vows that "Duesenberg will not die." But it did, just as Fred Duesenberg had died five years before, after sliding off the road in an SJ convertible, coming down Liginier Mountain in Pennsylvania. In this day, one would be as hard to resurrect as the other.

1935 Mercedes-Benz 500K Sports Roadster

1935 MERCEDES-BENZ 500K SPORTS ROADSTER

Engine Type: overhead valve in-line 8-cylinder, supercharged

Displacement: 4.9 liters (302 cubic inches)

Horsepower: 180

Transmission: 4-speed manual

Wheelbase: 129.5 inches

Overall Length: 206 inches

Overall Height: 63.7 inches

Overall Width: 69.2 inches

There isn't much to distinguish Loma Vista Drive from the other Truesdale streets as it climbs sharply up the south side of a Santa Monica mountain in Truesdale Estates near Los Angeles. However, it does differ in having two speed limits—25 mph for traffic going up and 15 mph for traffic coming down. There is a story behind them. One day a couple of years ago a runaway cement truck caromed down the curving road, blasting a big chunk out of a $200,000 house at the bottom of the hill and killing the driver. After that the downhill speed limit was reduced with lower gear usage specified for trucks.

Lestor Braunstein lives on Loma Vista Drive. He owns a fire engine red 1935 Mercedes 500K, with swoopy bodywork like the SS 100 Jaguar, only more massive. I had tracked it down after seeing it several times in traffic.

In the thirties the Mercedes was the natural rival of the Duesenberg, not just because it was foreign but because its design philosophy was different. Where the Duesenberg was a large, powerful, heavy automobile, the Mercedes was a smaller, powerful, lighter, better-handling car.

By 1934, while the Duesenberg was still largely a five-year-old design, except for the famous SJ 320 hp. supercharged engine that had been introduced, the Mercedes already had fully independent coil suspension and swing axles. The 500K was yet a further refinement with a 180 horsepower, supercharged, 302 cubic inch, in-line OHV eight-cylinder engine. Built on a 129-inch wheelbase (206-inch overall length) the Mercedes was not in the class of the 142.5- or 153.5-inch wheelbase Duesenberg.

You notice this immediately once the car gets under way. The three-passenger roadster is like all the great thirties' sporting cars: close-coupled, exuding the intimacy of an aircraft cockpit, with fine leather upholstery and a plethora of instruments. But, the car feels nimble and articulated, completely different from any U.S. car of the period. There is an audible moan from the 500K's four-speed transmission as the machine gathers speed. Steering is not exactly of the high level that we have come to expect of contemporary Mercedes, but it is a far cry from most of the other sporting rigs of its day.

Gliding through four lanes of Sunset Boulevard traffic without a lot of excitement, turning back occasionally to smile at the woman with blonde, windblown hair riding in the rumble seat, it might almost be 1935 again, though this early in the afternoon the homeward-bound flood of movie people would not have begun yet. But, encased in the 500K's arrogance—an arrogance possessed by only a handful of unique designs such as Rolls-Royce, Duesenberg, SJ, Mercer Type 35J Raceabout—it might almost be 1935. The giant flexible exhaust stacks shooting out of the engine compartment tell the onlooker this—the 500K is one of motoring's ultimate cars, right down to the "kompressor," the efficient, dead-descrip-

1935 Mercedes-Benz 500K Sports Roadster
Owner: Lester Braunstein   Photographed by Mark Madow

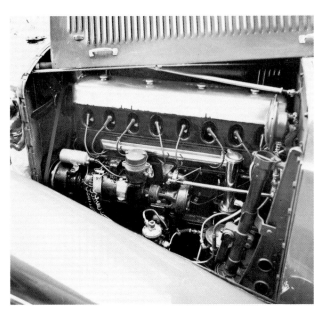

The 500K was powered by a 180-horsepower, supercharged, 302-cubic-inch, in-line, overhead-valve 8-cylinder engine.

tive German word for supercharger.

We press on. Past the ancient show-biz mecca of the hotel Chateau Maremont, where Tuesday Weld lives, and the place where the old Garden of Allah cottages once stood—where Scott Fitzgerald stayed on his first trip to Hollywood to write for the movies, and where Robert Benchley and Dorothy Parker swapped ripostes.

We find an open space in traffic and nail the accelerator. The big Merc leaps forward and the supercharger comes on like a brace of rocket launchers opening up. The carburetor works progressively and there is a narrow rpm band where the gas comes to the engine faster than it can be consumed. When that happens at night, a long tongue of yellow-red flame issues from the tailpipe.

Finally, we are climbing high up into the old Hollywood Hills, where these big elegant houses, homes with charm and character, are nestled into safe footholds on the slopes. We stop in front of a beautiful stone wall that forms the lower fortification for what seems like a late sixteenth-century chateau in the Loire Valley, and Madow, who has been following along in another car, goes to work. It is almost nightfall by the time the photo session is finished and the damp cold of the winter night has crept into the long shadows. We start back down toward the city with the top up and as we descend I know that Loma Vista Drive will never be like the old Hollywood Hills and that there will never again be cars like this.

1951 Nash Airflyte Ambassador Custom

1951 NASH AIRFLYTE AMBASSADOR CUSTOM

Engine Type: overhead valve in-line 6-cylinder

Displacement: 234 cubic inches (3.8 liters)

Horsepower: 115

Transmission: 3-speed manual with overdrive

Wheelbase: 121 inches

Overall Length: 211 inches

Overall Height: 62 inches

Overall Width: 77.5 inches

I had the keys to John Told's 1951 Nash Ambassador in my hand. In a city of nine million, we had had to scramble to find one. I pulled into the shop in a racy little Mercedes. And then I saw it; it had been years and I had forgotten just how big they were. Next to the Mercedes, the Nash looked like some strange, graceful Prairie Schooner from the past, a Jules Verne roadship. All seventeen feet, seven inches of it, weighing in at 3,445 voluptuously rounded pounds. Voluptuous in more ways than one, for the 1951 Nash Ambassador, the bathtub that turns into a bed, was perhaps the most obvious makeout car of all time.

As a teenager, I remember it being somewhat controversial. For a lot of girls, it was strictly off-limits. What father would let his daughter go to the drive-in in a car with seats that made into a bed? Very few, folks.

Whatever those Nash people were thinking of, they steered clear of any romantic possibilities in their ads. Those reclining seats were for sleeping, America, and nothing else.

In the 1951 Nash brochure there are nine photographs pointing out "All These Modern Advantages" of the new Nash.

Four of them refer carefully to the reclining seats.

The first shows a gray-haired man driving while his equally gray-haired wife sleeps primly on the reclined passenger seat.

Photo No. 2 shows two working-class heros driving in the countryside. One is driving and the other sleeps.

The third shows a grinning fisherman stretched out in the car, with all the slats down. Very practical.

And No. 4 goes after Motherhood. It shows mother and child sleeping peacefully while dad drives.

Just drop a latch, reads the ad, "to become a wonderfully comfortable daytime couch for sleepy children—yes, tired grown-ups, too." The only line that comes near to sexual innuendo reads, "Adjustable to five positions." But the implication from the bathtub's first appearance in 1949 was clear, especially to us sniggering adolescents. There were more Nash jokes than Polish jokes.

"Hey, I gotta date with Emily tonight. Know where I can borrow a Nash?" (Snort, snigger, guffaw.)

"The upholstery in my Nash gets worn out faster than the tires."

"What kind of mileage do I get? Six girls to the gallon."

It took courage to be single and drive a Nash. If you did, you were a "wolf."

But John Told wasn't thinking about love when he took the plunge into Nash ownership. He was thinking about blue jeans—and money. Some months ago, it came to John Told that with fashion focusing on the seedy natural uncombed look dependent on such high-fashion names as Levi, Lee, and Wrangler, there must be money in old denims. And he knew where there was a gold mine of jeans, back home in Orem, Utah—dirt-farmer country.

1951 Nash Airflyte Ambassador Custom
Owner: John Told   Photographed for *Motor Trend* by Mike Salisbury

So John went home in search of denims. In no time, John had rounded up 1,200 pounds of Levi pants and a number of jackets at a nickel apiece. In passing, he scrounged forty-five to fifty fur coats—aging silver fox furs and rabbit and who-knows-what—for $1 to $2 apiece. And, on a side trip to pick up some Indian jewelry, he found a four-foot, 300-pound dinosaur leg bone, which he couldn't resist at $75.

And then he heard about the Nash. "The grandfather of a friend of mine had died and left it behind, so I went out to look at it. It was sitting out in a barnyard field—it'd been there for about six months.

"I recognized it. I'd seen it for years around Orem. At church. I remember he had bought it brand new and always drove it to church. I'd been in it, too. I remember the ash tray was always full of gum wrappers and Certs wrappers. Mormons (Orem is a Mormon town) are against smoking, you know. Well, I had to have it. I just couldn't wait to get behind the wheel and light up a cigarette." Well, he figured that with 58,000 miles on the odometer and original paint, it couldn't be worth too much—in spite of the neat Sears, Roebuck seatcovers, and he got it for $75.

"It started right up. I couldn't believe it. It ran great. I found out the hard way that there wasn't any brake fluid in it. I was going about forty down this old dirt road and when I stepped on the brakes, nothing happened. Wow. It jumped a ditch, plowed through some four-by-four fencing and stopped in the middle of a herd of cows."

John took it home and began the ritual of polishing it. Underneath all that country dust and dirt was beauty. "All of a sudden it was beautiful. I bought the car just to bring back all those furs and Levis and the dinosaur bone. But after I cleaned the car up and drove it, I guess I fell in love with it."

Our country boy made out like Clyde Barrow on his business venture. He sold the nickel pants for two bucks apiece and the fur coats went for $25 to $40 each. Then he called the Museum of Natural History and asked if they might be interested in the leg bone of a dinosaur. Interested? They whipped off a check for $800. And when John Told, dressed stylishly in a worn Levis jacket, old knit sweater and shirt and faded Levi pants, drives his shiny Nash boat down shimmering Sunset Strip, people ask about buying that, too. "I used to get stopped about once a day by someone wanting to buy it. The highest bid was $800. But I think I'll keep it for the time being. I just drive it around town—no long trips."

And now here I was going for a test drive. Like someone who has found a secret attic in an ancient house, I opened the door slowly and got in. Gee, the seat is high. My God, how do I drive this battleship? The steering wheel is the size of a giant pizza pan. I turn and look out the rear window. Nothing. It's like looking down a long tunnel to where the light is. Okay, turn and hang your head out the window. Where does this car end? A Latino mechanic helps coach me out of the shop, and he's grinning all the way.

And now onto the street. The car gives a deep moan, then the half-moon speedometer with the strange numerals glides to 15 mph and I shift. It's about two feet on the column shift from first to second and now the moan matures to a cheerful hum as my ship of love picks up speed. I shift again, into third.

The car is so round and many-leveled that I'm not sure which lane I'm in. And there's enough slack in the steering wheel to weave a rug. I turn the wheel to turn the car, but it's still traveling straight ahead. I turn like crazy. Too much, it dips sideways like a schooner in a heavy trough, drifting suddenly to the left with all its weight. Egad, I'm on the edge of my seat. Will it come back? It does.

Look at all this space in here. If I were twenty-one again, I'd load this thing up with friends and beer and go roaring across the desert, radio blaring. You could play volleyball in here. From the windshield to the rear window, it's nine feet, four inches. It's more that six feet wide. At a stoplight, an old fellow in a baseball cap smiles, remembers.

Rolling up La Cienega Boulevard. You know, for a twenty-one-year-old car, it runs nicely, handsomely. Under that hood are 115 horses housed in a 234 cu. in. overhead valve engine. Six neat cylinders, all in a row. Vrooom, Vrooom. By Sunset and Laurel Canyon, I grow bold. I run it through the gears and it hums happily upward. Up into the High Sierra of L.A., the Hollywood Hills. Past baroque stucco homes lined with trees and shrubs, all soap-white, this humming blue bathtub rolls and pitches upward into the twilight. Higher, the pavement grows narrow, the homes sparse. Far up, sinking sun casts shadows below. The changing light

Sharon Taggart takes advantage of one of the Ambassador's
more controversial features.

bounces off hillside cottages, the sparse-grown trees and strangely pale blue waters in swimming pools.

And finally to the highest point in the hills. We round a corner and there's this megalopolis of Los Angeles, spreading out below us and stretching to the horizon.

It's photographed as the lights of the city come on. The blues of the Ambassador grow deeper, richer. I can't look at it on top of that hill without imagining a couple inside, necking—good old wholesome American necking.

The bathtub. That big, beautiful, romantic bathtub.

1963 Ferrari 250 GTO

1963 FERRARI 250 GTO

Engine Type: single overhead cam V-12

Displacement: 2.9 liters (174 cubic inches)

Horsepower: 300

Transmission: 5-speed manual

Wheelbase: 94.5 inches

Overall Length: 170 inches

Overall Height: 47 inches

Overall Width: 67 inches

When your average American talks about a GTO, it is usually safe to assume his conversation is about Pontiac's version. But when Pontiac dealers were confronted with the obvious question "What does G-T-O stand for?" they rarely knew, and those who did couldn't pronounce it: "Gran Turismo Omologato."

For further explanation you have to have a copy of the Federation Internationale de l'Automobile competition rule book for 1962. The prefix GT, of course, stands for Gran Turismo (or Grand Touring), while the suffix "O" is the Italian derivative of the verb "to homologate." Now for the purpose of definition, a car that is built to compete in a specific class and has met the requirements is said to be "homologated."

Whether or not the Ferrari 250 GTO was "homologated" was, at one time, quite a question. In 1952 the rules for the World Manufacturers Championship were changed, the emphasis shifting from the prototype cars to Gran Turismo. This meant that the automobiles competing must more closely resemble those sold for street use. The major requirement for homologation therefore, was that the manufac-

turer construct 100 examples. It was obvious to Ferrari that he could not build that number of his new cars, the 250 GTO, for the FIA's first review, so he applied on the somewhat suspect grounds that the GTO was an extension of his production 250 GT Berlinetta. It was a classic case of loophole shooting, a sport indulged in by all manufacturers. The illustrations that accompanied the GTO's papers showed the 250 GT and listed the various mechanical changes. A five-speed gearbox and dry-sump engine were the major differences. However, subtleties such as the Watts link in the rear suspension were numerous.

The new car was so fast and well balanced that it caused quite a stir with its competitors. It was loved by those who had one and hated by those who didn't. In the three years it competed in World Manufacturers Championship races (1962, '63, '64) it won the championship three times. Of the twenty-eight championship events held, the GTO Ferraris won twenty, finished second in fifteen and third in nine, and acquired a reputation for being virtually indestructible by finishing in approximately seventy percent of the events in which they were entered.

However, success in competition notwithstanding, it created another kind of rumpus behind the scenes. Its competitors saw the GTO as nothing more than a Testa Rossa with a roof. They demanded to know if the required 100 units had been constructed; in fact they raised an international stink about it. At the time the complaint was lodged only a handful had been built and over the entire three-year period only thirty-seven cars were completed. It was this fact that caused Aston Martin and Jaguar in particular to come off the wall. The irony of the situation was that both of these constructors had built similar lightweight/superfast ver-

In Retrospect

1963 Ferrari 250 GTO   Owner: Steven J. Earle

Photographed for Motor Trend by John Lamm

sions of their production cars in a lesser number than Ferrari had, a point generally ignored. It was just unfortunate they were so much slower. Carroll Shelby also got into the act because the ruckus made it that much harder to homologate the Cobra.

The GTO bodies were built by Scaglietti to a Pinin-Farina design. The Series I, or GTO '62-'63 cars were all constructed with two side vents and it is believed that aside from one or two cars the third vent was added after a car had received sufficient front-end damage for a rebuild.

Our subject car belongs to Steve Earle of Los Angeles and happens to be the finest GTO I have ever seen. It was completed on March 25, 1963 and delivered new April 22nd to Ecurie Nationale Belge. From there it was entered at Le Mans where it finished second overall driven by Jean Blaton "Berurlys" and Gerald Langlois Von Ophem. The car covered 2,700.8 miles at an average speed of 112.52 mph. With gas and oil it weighed 2,370 lbs. It is interesting to note that at Le Mans last year the class-winning 365 GTB-4 Daytona with its 4.4-liter engine only traveled 2,621.406 miles during the twenty-four hours.

Driving the GTO can best be described as sensual. To the racing driver of that period it was just another car, and "the bloody thing better go quickly." But to those of us who found our heroes out there the feeling is totally different. You're sitting in a seat that was reserved for people like Phil Hill, John Surtees and even Roger Penske.

Starting procedure is easy enough—depress the clutch, twist the key 360 degress, flip on the fuel pump, and as the tick, tick ticking slows down, stab the throttle a couple of times and push in on the ignition key. The variety of noises a Ferrari makes after going through the above procedure is difficult to describe. The engine

fires instantly and you are caught between engine and exhaust noise. You find yourself listening to the engine as though you had on stereo headphones—one end, then the other.

From the first snick of the gated gearbox the car is a delight to drive. It's a bit choppy but as speed picks up the ride becomes quite smooth. The only drawback is that the car was built for short-legged, long-armed Italians and this makes it difficult to operate the throttle and brake pedals at the same time. Your thigh locks in on the steering.

The GTO doesn't really begin to turn on until around 3,500 rpm, at which point all hell breaks loose. Zero to 60 mph is 6.1 seconds and the quarter-mile at 112 mph in 13.5 seconds. Try that on your Pontiac GeeTO.

Earle's car is twelve years old, and while its looks are becoming dated by its wire wheels and engine location (it was the last of the front-engined racing cars Ferrari built), it is surely one of the most beautifully proportioned automobiles built for any purpose. And it still provides one the ultimate driving pleasure, which is what Ferraris are all about. They may not be the best cars in the world, but surely they are the most exciting.

1928 Rolls-Royce Phantom I

1928 ROLLS-ROYCE PHANTOM I

Engine Type: overhead valve in-line 6-cylinder

Displacement: 7.6 liters (468 cubic inches)

Horsepower: Not from Rolls-Royce, thank you

Transmission: 3-speed manual

Wheelbase: 144 inches

Overall Length: 216 inches

Overall Height: 72 inches

Overall Width: 72 inches

"You must know Gatsby."

That line stopped me. I had known Gatsby—at least on paper. I remember tragedy, a love story, death, a mansion at West Egg on Long Island, noisy parties and, because of my preoccupation with automobiles, the Rolls-Royce. But I'd forgotten Gatsby's Rolls was a death weapon, the bridge between his dream and his demise.

Gatsby had to own a Rolls-Royce, in particular an American-made Rolls-Royce. Well-appointed Hispano-Suizas, Isotta-Frachinis, even Packards and Lincolns would have been respectable, but Gatsby, in his rush to attain everything that was thought to be the best, required himself to own a Rolls.

Paramount Pictures, makers of the current Gatsby film, specified an American version, a logical choice since the cars were built in Springfield, Massachusetts. Just after World War I, the English Rolls was suffering heavy import duty penalties and the mother company, drawing from the experience of its U.S. wartime aircraft engine plant, felt they could get the requisite quality materials and workmanship to

build their cars in the U.S. So, late in 1919, they started putting their stateside operation together, training locals in the proper method of building a Rolls. It wasn't until 1921 that any cars appeared.

They were all-American automobiles, but carbon copies of the British models, save for three points: the conversion to left-hand drive, a floor-mounted three-speed transmission (the British had four speeds), and the use in America of two coils in the dual ignition system instead of the British coil/magneto combination.

Silver Ghosts were built at Springfield from 1921 until 1926. The then-dated Ghost was replaced with the Phantom I, considered by many to be an interim model leading up to the Phantom II. As in the past, cars were offered complete (in Britain most were sold as bare chassis) using Brewster bodies, enough so that Rolls bought that coachworks in 1926. Gatsby's car would have been delivered in 1928 and properly called a Rolls-Royce Springfield Phantom I "Ascot." The more knowledgeable could have referred to it as a "Brewster Ascot" or "Speedster Phaeton." Gatsby would have paid $13,000 for the chassis and an additional $4,000 for the body. It shouldn't have mattered.

Today, the car belongs to Ted Leonard of Seekonk, Massachusetts (look just to the right of Providence, R.I.). When Paramount decided to use Leonard's car, he turned down any payment. Paramount insisted, so they settled on a dollar. He'll never cash the check. He commented that his car, chosen for the part at a Paramount-sponsored auto show in Newport, Rhode Island, was one of the few that could have been used by Gatsby. Most of the Phantom Is in the country were Springfield cars and the story requires that the car be open, yet able to become "an omnibus" bearing parties to and from the

RETROSPECT

1928 Rolls-Royce Springfield Phantom I Ascot
Owned by Mr. Ted Leonard
Photographed for *Motor Trend* by John Lamm

Nickel-silver flying lady radiator caps made in the U.S. (stamped U.S. PAT. OFF.) are very rare.

city between nine in the morning and long past midnight.

The long, open body was designed on a cocktail napkin by J.S. Inskip, president of Rolls-Royce in the U.S. The lines are a clean sweep, save for the usual accessory lights and the car doesn't look its 5,400 pounds. The radiator was a holdover from the Silver Ghost, as were the chassis, headlamps, and bumpers. There was nothing particularly spectacular about the body, except for the fact that it was bolted to a Rolls-Royce chassis.

The fenders on the car at the time it was photographed were made of fiberglass. The film's fatal accident involved denting the right front fender, so Paramount had a set of normal fenders reproduced and then made up a third fender with the appropriate dents. The book also prescribed a light-green interior, so the brown leather had to be dyed. The only other lasting effects of the filming were a few spots etched in the paint by the substance used for blood.

The interior was, as with most of the early, stately automobiles, wooden and simple. The closest thing to adornment is a row of Stewart-Warner gauges (said even by the British to have been of excellent quality) with Rolls-Royce imprinted on the faces. There were levers for such things as mixture and spark, levers that would mean nothing to most drivers in 1975.

Underneath the car was the massive frame you'd think Rolls would need to support such an

automobile. Of course, there were the Rolls idiosyncrasies—no rivets, thank you, tapered bolts will do. The four-wheel brakes got a boost from the transmission-mounted servo. The starter was on the transmission.

The engine was a six, with overhead valves and 468 cubic inches. Rolls was never so vulgar as to announce horsepower figures, but the automobile could hit 80 miles an hour. When Leonard had the engine overhauled, the forged crankshaft was found to have been made in England, the only non-American part in the powerplant.

Even the nickel-silver flying lady radiator cap, the crown of every Rolls-Royce, was made in the States. Each was a one-off from a wax cast, then plated by Gorham in Providence. In American tradition, though, even these reproductions of the Charles Sykes sculpture were stamped, "REG. U.S. PAT. OFF." Those letters make the American examples so rare (and thus valuable) that a phony was used during the filming.

The Rolls-Royce cars made in America outlasted Gatsby. He was gone before the thirties. Rolls lasted on Yankee soil until 1931 and the Depression. Which leads naturally to a question about this ancient Rolls' value. Paramount insured the car for $150,000 during the shooting of Gatsby, and Leonard concedes that he has received some surprisingly high offers for the car. Not that he cares. He claims that although he has owned hundreds of cars in his life, this is the first one his wife has liked.

1938 Buick "Y" Show Car

1938 BUICK "Y" SHOW CAR

Engine Type: overhead valve in-line 8-cylinder

Displacement: 320 cubic inches (5.2 liters)

Horsepower: 141

Transmission: 2-speed automatic

Wheelbase: 126 inches

Overall Length: 208 inches

Overall Height: 58 inches

Overall Width: 74 inches

It all began in the late 1930s. We were climbing out of a depression and digging our way into a war. Enrico Fermi was uncovering the mysteries of the atom. *Gone With the Wind* had just been made into a film, and FDR was well into his second term as president. And GM's Harley J. Earle, the man who put the profession of automobile designing on the map, had the envious privilege of driving to work in a brand-new special car that was the wildest thing on the road, bar none. It was called, simply, the Y-Job.

"I was completely amazed by it," says a designer who then was new to the firm's styling section. "For that time, it was fantastic." Built in 1938 and put on the road in 1939, the Y-Job had tremendous impact on auto design at several levels. It directly inspired the design of the 1942 Buicks, inside and out, with their low, sweep-fendered lines and wide grilles. The Y-Job was so sharp that a wire service reporter, spotting it by chance on the streets of Detroit in 1948, spread photos of it across the country identified as a sneak preview of the 1949 Buick! But the Y-Job's influence was not confined to

the U.S. In Italy, after the war, Piero Dusio, a wealthy businessman and car enthusiast, instructed the men who were to design a body for a car he wanted to build to make it look like a wider, lower version of the Buick, whose lines he liked very much. The designer was Pininfarina, and the car was the Cisitalia coupe, the gemlike foundation for all the finest postwar sports car shapes and styles. By then the Y-Job was semi-retired, pushed out of the spotlight in 1951 by a new generation of dream cars, the LeSabre and the Buick XP-300. Neither, however, was as profoundly influential as this long, black roadster with the curious name.

A giant of a man, both physically and professionally, Harley Earle had just begun to establish his styling section at GM in the late 1930s, under the protection of the head of the company, Alfred P. Sloan, Jr. One of the GM divisions that was most receptive to his styling ideas was Buick, which had been directed since 1933 by a super-salesman, Harlow H. Curtice. In 1936 the Flint-based division acquired an enthusiastic new chief engineer, Charles A. Chayne. These were men who knew what Earle was talking about when he proposed radical changes in the shapes of future Buicks.

Earle turned to Buick late in 1937 when he needed support for the construction of a radical special car to serve two purposes. It was to be a trial horse for some new car styling ideas, and it was also to be a personal car for Earle himself, a supreme showman. "I want a nice little semi-sports car," Earle told a small cadre of designers, "a kind of convertible." He wanted it as low as possible, recalls Vince Kaptur, Sr., on whose years of experience Earle relied to bring his ideas to life.

"We were always working with X-cars, for experimental purposes," remembers Kaptur,

RETROSPECT

1938 Buick "Y" Show Car
Owned by General Motors
Photographed for *Motor Trend* by John Lamm

"and this job was one step beyond that. We just called it the Y-Job." Kaptur was in charge of the body engineering of this one-off car, with assistance from John Parks on the machinery details. George Snyder, an exceptionally capable stylist, was the man who interpreted Earle's desires and drew the lines that defined the Y-Job.

The creation had a classically tapered nose and modified boat-tail rear deck, blended together in a sleek central fuselage unmarred by moldings or running boards. Blended into the main form, in a manner that looks smooth and simple now but was exceptional then, were firmly tapered front and rear fender forms. Skirts were integral with the fenders at the rear, as emphasized by the fine chrome stripping covering them, and the bold vertical trailing edge of each fender was new, a subtle precursor of the finned era.

The front end design of the Buick-based Y-Job broke completely away from vertical orientation. The grille was entirely horizontal, with a pleasing rounded contour and vertical bars that were inspired by the grille of the just-introduced 1938 Mercedes-Benz W154 Grand Prix car. The grille was given center stage, too, by a novel hidden-headlight system. In front of each light was a circular lid split horizontally so its two sections blinked open, up and down, like eyelids whenever the lights were switched on. Echoing the grille shape on the original Y-Job were the flared tips of the fenders. At first it had bumper guards like those introduced on 1941 Buicks, and the basic bumper shape appeared on the '42 models. After the war, the car was fitted with stock 1946 Buick bumpers, which it still has.

No lightweight, with its steel body and chrome-plated bronze brightwork, the Y-Job rolled on a 1938 Buick Century chassis with a 126-inch wheelbase. That was Buick's first year with all-coil suspension and and an improved straight-eight engine—"Dynaflash" in the jargon of the era. From 320 cubic inches it developed 141 bhp at 3,600 rpm. Early in its career, the Y-Job was equipped with a prototype of the Dynaflow torque converter transmission that became a Buick option in 1948. This roadster measured 208 inches in length, 74 inches in width and 58 inches in overall height—very low for its time.

The Y-Job's dash also was a pacesetter for future Buicks, with its central speedometer, clear round dials and minor controls built into the decorative bars across the radio speaker grille. Two of the dash switches were push buttons controlling another pioneering feature of the Y-Job: electric power windows. Another pair of push buttons operated the convertible top. This was also electric, a complicated machine that automatically raised and lowered the rear-deck cover while the top was moving up or down. The seat was a pleated bench design, and the big accelerator pedal had its heel deeply recessed into the floorboard to give extra legroom for the lanky Earle.

Cranks worked the opening quarter-windows in the doors. The only other inside door controls were lock buttons and a push button that opened the door. This and a similar button on the outside of each door opened the latch electrically. It was rigged so that an extra-hard push would open the door latch mechanically if the electricity went on strike. To open the rear deck you turned a key in a lock at the back, causing a flush-fitting handle to pop out. Turning that opened the tapered lid, which uncovered a spare tire and little room for anything else.

Of two novel chassis features tried in the Y-Job, one was successful—power steering, a Bendix unit built according to the designs of Francis W. Davis. Buick was the first GM division to get excited about power steering's potential. It had made firm plans to introduce it as an option on the '42 models but two gentlemen named Hitler and Tojo caused second thoughts about that. Not until the 1950s did the Y-Job's power steering become widely available.

Another experimental system didn't make the grade. This was a novel drum brake that used a bladder, instead of the usual cylinder, to press the linings against the drum. A derivative of a brake design that had worked in aircraft, it was a flop in the Y-Job. When it worked, it didn't slow this heavy car very effectively, and the bladder also could burst and put the brakes right out of commission. That happened once in Georgia to Leonard McVay, whose job it became after the war to keep the Y-Job rolling. One reason these brakes were tried was that the Y-Job had thirteen-inch wheels, minuscule by 1938 standards. The wheel discs had louvered slots intended to help cool the brakes, and the tire size was 7.00 x 13.

The major significance of the Y-Job, however, lay in its overall proportions. During the 1930s, Earle had led the fight to move the automobile's passenger compartment forward, where it

would be better placed between the wheels, and downward. Unlike the classic roadster, which was all hood, the Y-Job had a rear deck that was longer than the hood. In the major auto companies it set a trend toward shorter hoods and longer rear decks that prevailed until the early 1960s. Always intrigued by aircraft, Earle was certainly influenced by their proportions in his successful drive to transform the profile of the automobile. Since then, of course, cars like the Mustang and the Grand Prix have led the return to the more spectacular but far less functional long-hood look.

There was no glamorous press introduction for the Y-Job, no round of motor show appear-ances. Weathered in by the gloom of a depression and the lowering clouds of war, America wasn't much interested in auto shows when the Y-Job was completed in 1939. It became instead a sales tool for Earle, who put many miles on it during and after the war years at his homes in Grosse Pointe and Florida. But with the Y-Job as his springboard, Earle succeeded in the 1940s and early 1950s in transforming the shape of the American car. And when, in 1951, the Y-Job was rolled out for comparison with Earle's next dream machine, the Le Sabre, everyone could trace the new car's parentage to this proud black classic roadster.

1931 Ruxton Roadster

1931 RUXTON ROADSTER

Engine Type: L-head in-line 8-cylinder

Displacement: 286 cubic inches (4.6 liters)

Horsepower: 85

Transmission: 3-speed manual

Wheelbase: 130 inches

Overall Length: 183.5 inches

Overall Height: 41.6 inches (to top of door)

Overall Width: 68.3 inches

Whatever happened to the Ruxton? It seems to be the great mystery classic car. None of the few articles written about it agree on every detail. The plotting and finagling around the production of the Ruxton reads like a file from the Securities and Exchange Commission and no one even agrees about how many were built. About the only general consensus is that the Ruxton was an excellent automobile caught in less than excellent times—the Depression. At any rate, here is the Ruxton's story, as near as can be determined.

With what proved to be a certain amount of melodramatic irony, the Ruxton started as a prototype called the Question Mark. At least that was on the radiator badge of the front-wheel-drive sedan that circulated through the streets of New York City in 1929.

William J. Muller, the car's designer, was a self-educated engineer, schooled at America's rough pre-World War I auto racetracks. After the war, he joined the Edward G. Budd Company, producers even today of automobile body panels. In his job as a developmental engineer, Muller thought Budd should build a front-drive

"idea car" with production potential. He went to Budd with the idea, got an allocation of $15,000 and after two years and a total of $35,000, the car was ready to drive.

Muller turned a Studebaker six-cylinder engine around in the chassis and bolted it up to a Warner gearbox. A differential was grafted to the back of the transmission, Spicer constant velocity universal joints got the power through halfshafts to the wheels, and Muller had his front-drive.

It was a low machine, much lower than most anything else in that era of huge automobiles. In fact, there wasn't even a need for running boards. Budd liked the car, but their business was bodies, not complete automobiles. Now they needed a manufacturer.

Enter Archie Andrews. Here was Horatio Alger, circa 1929, a financier and promoter building a fortune in the wide-open American business community of the twenties. Some say that he was worth $50 million by 1929. Through his money, Andrews had gotten on the boards of directors of several corporations, including Dictagraph, Trans-Lux, Hupp (makers of the Huppmobile) and, finally, Budd. The pieces were falling into place.

Andrews liked Muller's Question Mark and in mid-February he swung a deal to take over the car from Budd to build and market it. All he needed was a company to produce it, a seemingly minor point to a man like Andrews. He had planned on taking the car over to Hupp for manufacture, but was shut off by the president of that firm. In the meantime, he was talking to private investors about starting his own company.

One of those he talked to was William V.C. Ruxton. Andrews named the new car after Ruxton, hoping, no doubt, to gain his favor and

RETROSPECT

1931 Ruxton Roadster
Owner: Dr. William O'Brien III
Photographed for *Motor Trend* by John Lamm

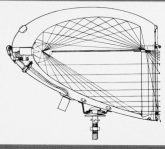

his finances. It didn't work and Mr. Ruxton dropped out. Andrews still didn't have any investors, but at least he had a name for his car.

Having failed twice, Andrews set up his own firm with Muller, the point being to find some way to get the Ruxton into production. Ironically, he named his new company New Era Motors, Inc. Muller went to work on the first production prototype.

This car—some say it was a converted Huppmobile—was even more exciting than the Question Mark. The Studebaker engine was swapped for a Continental straight-eight turned around for front-wheel drive. Muller wanted to shorten the driveline package and thus the hood. He discarded the Warner gearbox and designed his own transaxle. He split the transmission, putting first and reverse ahead of the differential, with second and high between the differential and the clutch. Then, he replaced the conventional ring and pinion final drive with a worm gear and wheel unit. This combination cut almost a foot off the driveline length. Spicer constant velocity U-joints were used in the front halfshafts.

Like the Question Mark, the Ruxton protoype was low. It had no running boards, and the hood was not much higher than the fenders—which, in 1929, was dynamite.

With the prototype built, the promotion began. There were photos, demonstration rides, promises that 12,000 cars would be built in the remaining months of 1929—everything, alas, but a place to build the car. At this point, the world began to turn to gruel in Andrews's hands.

First, Fred Gardner, who made an automobile bearing his name, announced that he would build the Ruxton. The deal fell through. So Andrews went to Marmon to see if they would build it. Colonel Howard Marmon drove the car, liked it immediately, and wanted to start production. That arrangement was washed away with the stock market. Andrews's frustration was rising.

Next, the Moon Company announced they would build the Ruxton. More accurately, they needed the car to stay alive. Their Moon and Diana models were dying in the showrooms and the Ruxton seemed a way back. So Moon traded New Era a majority of their outstanding common stock (accounts vary between 52 and 68 percent) for rights to the Ruxton. Too late, the Moon executives saw Andrews lining up for a takeover. To block it, there was a merger with Gardner to strengthen their position. When Andrews requested a seat on the board, they refused him. Andrews, understandably irate, headed for St. Louis with a court order. The Moon executives barricaded themselves in the factory with armed guards. Andrews and his force had to climb through to get in and take control.

For all that, Moon was a poor place to build a car. The factory was set up to sell "assembled" cars, but not to manufacture parts. Of course, the irrepressible Andrews had another ace to play: Kissel Motor Company. He had advanced a loan to George Kissel and his Hartford, Wisconsin, plant seemed the place to build the Ruxton. Muller inspected the plant and gave it his recommendation. It seemed that at long last the gods had been aligned and the Ruxton would be built in numbers using both the Moon and Kissel factories. No such luck.

Through all this hassling and scrambling, the country's economy was grinding down. In the history of the automobile, there has probably never been a worse time than 1929 to introduce an automobile, much less one that cost $4,500. There were orders, of course. They had been piling up since the Ruxton was first introduced by Andrews, but now Kissel was in trouble. Mortgage payments were missed and rather than have the company fall into Andrews's hands, George Kissel asked that the company be placed in receivership. Since all the tooling for the final drive assembly was tied up at Kissel, Moon had to close down when their supply ran out. Andrews was still a wealthy man, but he could see he was pouring good money down a dry hole. The frustration ended in New Era's bankruptcy in December 1930.

Perhaps the most frustrating part of the story is that the Ruxton deserved to make it. Andrews wasn't chasing a flippant idea or a freak car. The engineering community applauded Muller's efforts and early orders had shown that the car would sell.

The front-drive had already captured the public's imagination in Harry Muller's race cars. Extensive road tests of the Ruxton eliminated any fears of shimmy or wheel fight. A distribution of the sedan's 4,000 pounds as 53 percent front and 47 percent rear helped belay the rumors that front-drive cars lost traction on steep hills. A favorable ratio of sprung to unsprung weight meant good ride and

The "Woodlite" headlamps, said to have been designed to reduce glare, helped the Ruxton stand out from the crowd.

The front axle had Spicer constant velocity universal joints.

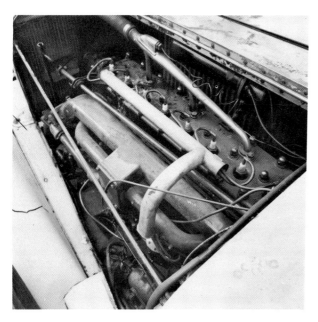

The 18-horsepower engine was turned backwards and the exhaust pipe routed forward, down, and back to a muffler under the engine.

roadholding.

By 1930, the car was using Continental's 18S engine. Horsepower was 85 at 3,000 rpm from 268 cubic inches. Because the engine was turned backwards, the exhaust pipe was routed forward, down and back to a muffler under the engine. With most of the engine pieces on the left of the powerplant (and with little room under the floorboards of the low car) the battery was moved up under the hood—quite a feature in 1929.

Besides the front-drive halfshafts, the front had a fairly normal I-beam axle, bent forward in the middle to clear the transmission housing. The rear axle was made of a carbon steel tube and both axles were sprung with semi-elliptics. Lockheed hydraulic brakes were used.

But it was the esthetics that made the Ruxton. Remember that in 1929, prestige automobiles were, for the most part, quite tall. The Ruxton was as low as 63-1/4 inches. As one might expect, the body panels for the sedans were actually modified panels from what was to have been a model of the British Wolseley. The roadsters were made by the Raulang Body Company.

One feature that always helped the Ruxton stand out were the "Woodlite" headlamps. They were said to have been designed to reduce glare. The bulb was placed high in the lamp, right at the strip around the upper part of the fixture. Light was reflected and focused through the lamp and lens as a flat beam. In fact, it was so well focused at one point on the lens that it is said you could light a cigarette at the point where the beams intersected. They never really met the approval of the state highway officials, though, and never came into popular use.

In the end, it was all for nothing. The Woodlites, Muller's transaxle, and Andrews's enthusiasm all went kaput in 1930. When they finally locked the doors, 316 cars had been built. Of that number, only 19 exist today. (That figure is the estimate of Jack Dolan in a letter to *Classic Car*.)

Agajanian Willard Special 1963 Indianapolis Winner

AGAJANIAN WILLARD SPECIAL
1963 INDIANAPOLIS WINNER

Engine Type: dual overhead cam in-line 4-cylinder
Displacement: 251.9 cubic inches (4.1 liters)
Horsepower: 400 (approx.)

If you were at the Indianapolis 500 a dozen years ago, you probably drove home asking yourself, "I wonder if that was right, if Jones really won that race?"

You had just seen Rufus Parnel (Parnelli) Jones win a controversial race in one of the most famous Indy cars of all time—the A.J. Watson-built, number 98 roadster owned by J.C. Agajanian. Jones called the car "Ol' Calhoun" and both became almost infamous by winning the '63 Indy 500.

Controversy, you see, has somehow always been part and parcel of the Brickyard. It isn't planned. In fact, it's carefully planned against by the United States Auto Club (the organization that sanctions the event) and by the guys who run the venerable Indianapolis Motor Speedway. Yet each year the protests fall as heavily and as certainly as the rains that always come during those frantic thirty days in May.

In the closing stages of the '63 race, USAC officials were about to put a halt to Jones' race because Calhoun was leaking oil. The race starter, Pat Vidan, had actually picked up the black flag and was awaiting word from Chief Steward Harlan Fengler. Serious business. They were going to wave the race leader to a complete standstill in the pits (for an inspection of his car), thus virtually giving the race to a rookie who was running second in a very funny-looking car.

The rookie was a guy named Jim Clark and he wasn't driving an Offenhauser-powered roadster and the '63 Indy was his first American oval track event. That Clark had been world champion and that cars like his mid-engine Lotus-Ford were clearly the wave of the future may have been factors in Fengler's eventual decision.

As Calhoun's owner, Agajanian, saw Vidan pick up the black flag, he angrily clamped down on his ten-gallon Stetson hat and quick-stepped it toward the steward's stand on the high heels of $300 cowboy boots. Aggie was furious and Aggie was (and remains) an imposing man in the pits, garages, and behind the scenes at Indianapolis—or wherever the proud championship cars are raced.

When Aggie got to the officials' stand, he and Fengler, once known as "the boy wonder of the board tracks," had a monumental confrontation. Aggie, remember, brought his first car to Indy in 1948. He tasted victory there in '52, when 22-year-old Troy Ruttman became the youngest driver ever to win USAC's premier event. But it had been an 11-year drought since Aggie had doffed his Stetson in Victory Lane. And he wasn't getting anywhere with Fengler. Meanwhile, Jones and Calhoun kept circling the field, leading the race.

The fans were accustomed to seeing Calhoun out front. For the second year in a row, Jones had put it on the pole—only three other men had taken the pole at Indy two years running: Ralph DePalma, Rex Mays, and Eddie Sachs. And,

1963 Indianapolis Winner Agajanian Willard Special
Driven by Parnelli Jones Photographed by John Mahoney

since 1952, the entire front row at Indy had been filled by Offy-powered cars. In '63, that changed. Jim Hurtubise put one of the now-revered, Andy Granatelli Novis into the No. 2 starting spot. These were supercharged double-overhead cam V-8s, fast enough to have captured the pole position in past 500s and, as the race proved, still fast enough for Hurtubise to lead and then run second for thirty-eight laps.

Elsewhere in the field were the two "White Owl" Lotus-Fords, driven by Dan Gurney and Jimmy Clark. Looking like cigars on wheels, the Lotuses used engines patterned after the 260 cu. in. stock-block Ford passenger car engines and ran along quite nicely, thank you, on everyday, ordinary gasoline. If the Novis were the faint sweet smell of the past (and they were), the Lotus-Fords were the future and that was more than obvious as Clark motored sedately along in Jones' and Calhoun's wake through the latter stages of the '63 500.

Calhoun was a dinosaur, a hybrid evolutionary hothouse violet—sturdy, predictable, gawdalmighty fast down the chutes, and, alas, a handful in the four distinctly different turns that make up the 2-1/2-mile Indy oval.

Calhoun's lineage could be traced back some 40 years to the high-boy, rocking horse, championship dirt track cars that were the mainstay of professional auto racing in the U.S. for the first fifty years of this century. For years, Indianapolis was the only paved track (brick being the surface until 1935, when the track was paved for the first time) on the championship car schedule. The cars that raced at Indy also raced in the dirt of other events. The last multi-purpose car to win Indy was Aggie's '52 car, driven by Ruttman.

The next evolutionary stage was the roadster (mostly built by—or copied from—a fellow named Frank Kurtis) and Calhoun was perhaps the finest roadster ever built. It was A.J. Watson's creation. Tall, lean, and businesslike, Watson, like Agajanian, came to Indy for the first time in 1948. He began building his own cars two years later. By '63, you expected an A.J. Watson-built car to win, and sometimes the entire front row was made up of them. His cars had finished one-two in three previous 500s and had dominated the race since 1955. (To this day, you can find Watson roadsters running as Supermodified on half-mile tracks all over America.)

In '63, Calhoun had been given only cosmetic changes since it rolled out of Watson's Burbank shop in 1960. Veteran Indy car metal man Eddie Kuzma had spruced up the wide aluminum body panels with a few flares and scoops, but underneath it was all Watson. The chassis was (and remains to this day—in the Speedway Museum where the car is on display) a space frame design utilizing 1-1/2-inch chrome moly tubing that is gusseted like the Eiffel Tower—or a Mercedes 300SL, if you prefer.

With the body panels field-stripped, you wonder at the rugged, cross-torsion bar suspension (both fore and aft) that tied onto solid axles. Plenty strong stuff. The torsion bar arms weigh about six pounds apiece. One man would have a rugged time installing the Halibrand rear end. (For the technically oriented, it is a three-inch, open-tube style with double spot brakes at each wheel.) The entire package weighed about 1,600 pounds.

Calhoun was a 96-inch-wheelbase roadster and they hung big 16-inch wheels on the front and 18-inchers in the rear. The rubber on Calhoun, like most Indy cars of the era, was from Firestone. The first rhubarb of the month, however, revolved around rubber. The Lotus-Ford showed up with fifteen-inch wheels and Goodyear rubber and then Mickey Thompson showed with twenty-two mechanics and five Buick-powered, rear-engine cars that featured twelve-inch wheels. Parnelli bolted a set of fifteen-inchers on Calhoun and went even faster, but there really wasn't any difference in either tire size, on the dinosaurs.

The highest part of a roadster, the windshield, was about hip-high to a tall Indian. It looked like you'd need a stepladder simply to climb into the thing. And, in '63, Indy cars had exhaust pipes on them—not just dinky, little tubes sticking out of snail-like headers wrapped around and around the back end of the car, but big, swoopy, chrome-plated, three-inch jobs giving the old Offy mills an unmistakable, bellicose drone.

The cars were sanitary, too. Big and bulky though they were, everything was contained within the car's skin. There were no coolers (oil, transmission) or other plumbing gadgets hanging off every corner. And they got by without wings and "aerodynamic" things. From the grandstands, you could actually see Parnelli wrestling that hulk through Indy's nearly flat turns. Roadsters required shoulders and room to move them in.

The engine in Calhoun was offset some seven

inches, to equalize things for left-turn-only racing. The driveshaft ran alongside Jones' left leg. He sat in an old aircraft-style bucket seat, bolt upright, and the seat back wrapped around his ribcage on the right, presumably to help hold him in an upright position. The wrap-around seat was called a "granny" and drivers don't hold that as an assault on their manhood. The roadsters steered hard in those days and arm exercises were the rage in Gasoline Alley. Roadsters were brutes.

But in the late stages of the '63 500, the one the

At the start of the 1963 Indy 500, Parnelli Jones in Calhoun is at the far right. Jim Clark's Lotus is the low-slung slender auto in the middle of the pack.

brute Calhoun was leading while Aggie and Harlan Fengler invoked the gods along pit row—Calhoun was really spilling oil by then. Suddenly, driver Eddie Sachs (the guy they called the "Clown Prince" of car racing, the guy who would die a year later in a fiery crash on the second lap) was spinning—on oil. Out of the race. Then, with one lap to go, Roger McCluskey looped it, on oil, while running in third, behind Clark.

Then the race was over. And the anger burbled over in the pits because Pat Vidan had never raised that black flag. USAC officials checked the oil level in Calhoun's tank and found it to be ample. There was just a little crack in it and, once the oil level fell below that point, why, it stopped leaking . . . or so the story goes. (Another one goes that a quick, crafty Aggie crew member dumped oil into the tank as the car was pulled into Victory Lane.)

So, Calhoun won the '63 Indy 500.

You may be wondering what it was that Aggie said to Fengler that day in May a decade ago. They're not talking; except for Aggie, who allows that he fought for his team and won. Even the most Marquis of Queensbury sportsman would have to agree that Ol' Calhoun was worth fighting for, that it would have been a shame if the car that led the race three times (in 1962 when the brakes went out and in 1964 when it caught on fire during a routine refueling stop) never won it.

And Parnelli? Well, "Ol' P.J.," as they call him now, won $148,000 and change out of that half-million-buck purse of '63. He listened to Aggie, invested his money wisely and somewhere along the line he even took a Dale Carnegie course. Today he manages the "Super Team" of Championship Car racing and he, (along with Mario Andretti, Al Unser, and Joe Leonard—totaling five Indy wins between them) will be back again this year at Indy, trying for the largest hunk of a purse that's gone up to a cool million in the last decade.

You've got to figure he stops by the Speedway Museum and gives Calhoun a good fond pat every year. Together, they were the best of an era and even held back the future—for just a little while, a decade ago.

4 1/2-Liter Blower Bentley

4½-LITER BLOWER BENTLEY

Engine Type: single overhead cam in-line 4-cylinder, supercharged

Displacement: 4.3 liters (267.7 cubic inches)

Horsepower: 240

Transmission: 4-speed manual

Wheelbase: 130 inches

Overall Length: 175 inches

Overall Height: 54 inches

Overall Width: 68.5 inches

Somehow, we weren't ready for the 4-1/2-liter Blower Bentley sitting there idling at 350 rpm, half in Phil Hill's driveway and half out into the street. The car was too small. It looked like a racing sports car, not the lumbering British duplicate of a late '20's Lincoln or Cad with cycle fenders we had expected. All through these years, with only the pictures from Le Mans and Brooklands, and Pau and who knows where else, the Bentleys attained ponderous dimensions in our minds. But they are, in fact, maybe the neatest high-performance road cars ever designed—the wire mesh over the radiator and headlamps; the Amherst Villiers, Rottes-type supercharger jutting out like some kind of medieval war engine between the frame's dumbirons.

Never mind that this particular Bentley configuration failed to win a major race in its abbreviated two-and-a-half-year career because that's not what is important. Just remember that Tim Birkin, the gentleman who masterminded the whole Blower deal, finished second in the 1930 French GP at Pau, *with a two-and-a-*

half-ton touring car! That and the fact that the thing will still go 125 with the screen flat and the hood (top) down make this a notable car.

It isn't like Duesenberg almost winning LeMans or Stutz almost winning Le Mans. The normally aspirated Bentleys, the 3-liter four, the 4.5-liter four and, later, the 6.5-liter "Speed Six" won in 1924, '27, '28, '29, and '30. Bentleys didn't need a supercharger. In fact, the old man, W.O. Bentley himself, never liked blowers because they were the antithesis of his priorities; he concentrated "first on reliability, then on smoothness and silence, and lastly on sheer power output."

The Bentleys were a spin-off of that fantastic, halcyon time between the great wars when anything in England was still possible. Created in the precise, mechanical mind of W.O. Bentley, who designed the rotary engine for the Nieuport Scout fighters, the cars fit exactly the preoccupations of the superrich looking for an act to follow WWI. Like some kind of ultimate in-club, the Bentley Boys—Tim Birkin, Glen Kidston, Woolf Barnoto, J. Dudley Benjafield, S.C.H. "Sammy" Davis, L.G. Callingham—and an elite supporting cast, bought their Bentley cars from the factory for the privilege of racing these same cars on the factory team. Eccentric perhaps, but you must remember that the Bentleys were the Porsche 917s of their day.

Bentley's dedication to reliability meant there was nothing tricky about his cars. The high-grade steel ladder frames were exceptionally deep-section, with four pressed-steel, and three tubular steel, crossmembers. Even with this, the frame's extreme length made it somewhat flexible. Like the Mercer Raceabout, the four-speed Bentley transmission was not fitted directly to the engine, mounted instead about a foot-and-a-half back, between two crossmem-

In Retrospect

4½-Liter Blower Bentley   Owner: Phil Hill

bers. Worm and sector steering is used and it's still accurate with good road feel.

The engine's four cylinders are cast in one block with a non-detachable head on which the camshaft is cradled by seven bearings. The crankshaft rode in eight.

Bentley designed a four-valve arrangement because the exhausts ran cooler; that and "for the same valve acceleration, you get much quicker opening." The camshaft is driven by three connecting rods coupled to a three-throw crankshaft at the rear of the engine crank. With

two S.U. carburetors the engine produces 125 h.p. at 3,500 rpm.

But, as mighty as the carburetored cars were, the supercharger's siren call led the most flamboyant of the Bentley Boys, Tim Birkin, to seek out Charles Amherst Villers to rig a blower setup for a separate team. The sheer magnitude of the power gain from 125 hp at 3,500 rpm to 235 hp at 4,200 rpm was impressive, but so were the strains on the engine. Time after time the Blower Four-and-a-Halves had their own race way out in front of the field somewhere,

The Bentley engine's four cylinders are cast in one block with a nondetachable head on which the camshaft is cradled by seven bearings.

breaking and rebreaking the track record, only to expire from one ailment or another. (Bentley believed these failures destroyed the public's confidence in his other cars, and in part, led to the company's demise.)

Phil came out of the house and we climbed up three feet into the car on the passenger side. There is no door for the driver. You sit down next to the floor like in a modern sports car, your legs angled only slightly. The 39-inch-wide upholstered leather cockpit is classically narrow, but not claustrophobic. The driver and passenger are involved in a way not possible in our own era of consoled-off compartments.

From inside you don't get the distinct metallic rhythm of 16-rocker-arm actuated valves. The engine noise just melds into a kind of low mechanical whir of rods and aluminum pistons ramming their way up and down the quart-oil-can-sized 3.94-inch diameter cylinder bore. Phil pulled the shift-lever into low and there was a subdued gnashing of unsynchronized, straight-cut gear; gears that scream-whine up through first and second and third like a 10,000-watt stereo-amplified Chevy Warner T-1. But not fourth, the only thing you really get in high is the low boom of the storm-drain-sized exhaust pipe.

We were on our way now, down to the Pacific Coast Highway. We got off Pacific Coast Highway on Tuna Canyon, a narrow, corrugated, twisted asphalt ribbon that winds up into the wild Santa Monica Mountains behind Malibu. "I'll tell you one thing," Phil said as we negotiated a small flurry of curves, "you've got to pay attention to what you're doing. Just like a motorcycle, you've got to keep your eyes open miles ahead because you get going so much faster than the rest of the car is capable of keeping up with. With these little skinny tires, this thing is sideways before other people know they're cornering. When the car goes 'round a corner, the weight transfer is enormous.

"You come into a bumpy turn too fast, boy, you're in for a thrill. The frame just becomes one huge, undamped spring flapping in all directions."

Somewhere along the crest of one of the hills, we stopped to get set up for some running shots. Phil said he would go back around the last turn and come on at moderate speed. We heard the car start to pick up speed and almost before we realized it, he burst from the corner at full song, tires howling, and swung in a graceful flat drift, power on, tail put out just so, through the shallow curve before us. For that one instant we knew what the Bentley Boys and a Blower Four-and-a-Half were all about.

Auburn Model 851 Speedster

AUBURN MODEL 851 SPEEDSTER

Engine Type: L-head in-line 8-cylinder, supercharged

Displacement: 279.2 cubic inches (4.5 liters)

Horsepower: 150

Transmission: 3-speed manual

Wheelbase: 127 inches

Overall Length: 205 inches

Overall Height: 58 inches

Overall Width: 78 inches

In 1924 the Auburn Automobile Company of Auburn, Indiana, lost $70,000 and found Errett Lobban Cord. Actually, there's a little confusion as to who found whom. We do know that the Chicago bankers who controlled Auburn installed twenty-nine-year-old Cord as vice president and de facto head of the faltering company that year. Three years later, Cord was president of Auburn and the company turned a profit of a million bucks.

The first order of business for Cord at Auburn was to unload some 800 unsold touring cars that were cluttering up the books and the fields around the plant. He accomplished this feat by tarting up the old boats with some flashy paint and chrome trim and hustling them out of there like the spellbinder he was. His method was prophetic, taking pretty undistinguished machines and clothing them with the appearance of something out of the ordinary, then peddling them to the proles with all the zeal and hyperbolic hustle of a carnival press agent. Selling the sizzle instead of the steak; it would become the pattern for most of Cord's automotive activities during the next ten or twelve

years. One could be uncharitable and say that Cord set the pattern for the entire domestic automotive industry in this respect, except that his cars did look conspicuously different from their contemporaries, and they were invariably executed with great taste and style.

The Auburn Model 851 Speedster shown here probably represents the high-water mark for zesty, unusual-looking cars in America. It was produced in 1935 and '36, and certainly nothing so spectacular has come off an American production line since. The Auburn Speedster probably wasn't a great car by the usual standards, but it was a great-looking car by any standard, and an incredible value for the money. The Speedster was decked out with an impressive array of mechanical gadgetry, including a Schwitzer centrifugal supercharger and a Columbia two-speed rear axle. It had the startling Buehrig-designed boat-tail body, virtually handmade; a top speed guaranteed to be over a hundred miles per hour; and you could buy one—signed, sealed, and delivered—for a mere $2,245. A steal. And yet, with the Depression and all, they only sold 500 of the big old beauties. A tragedy.

In 1942 I had this recurrent pre-erotic fantasy. I would be walking along the streets of Royal Oak, Michigan, folding the *Detroit Free Press* and throwing it onto people's roofs or into their bushes, and this lovely chick about my age, 11, would suddenly dart into the street and tumble into the path of an onrushing transit-mix cement truck. I would drop my paper bag and snatch her from the jaws of death, whereupon her rich, grateful father would reward me with her hand in marriage, a free college education, and a new Auburn Speedster every year for the rest of my life. You can imagine my dismay when I learned that Auburn had closed its doors

forever not long before my sixth birthday.

It's instructive, thirty years later, to examine a shiny, like-new Auburn Model 851 Speedster, the car that figured so prominently in those paper route reveries. It is one huge mother, and the overall feeling of heft and bulk is repeated and amplified by every piece of equipment on the car—except for the Crosley radio and heater, which look like miniature scale models of themselves. It's so big, and so yellow, that you don't quite know how to approach it. So you stand about twenty feet away, at first, and say a lot of heavyweight automotive expert stuff like "Oh, wow" and "Jee-zuss!"

There's this radiator grille that appears to come to about your shoulder. It looks like a chrome-plated streamlined sled for Buck Rogers's kids stuck on the front. Big old bulb headlights that say "STABILITE HEAD LAMP" on the lenses eyeball you as you stand there, and right there in the upper middle of the radiator shell, reading from top to bottom in raised letters that must have blown the art directors' minds at the Century of Progress Exhibition, it says "A-U-B-U-R-N." It would have been a privilege to be mowed down by one of those dudes and lie in state at the mortuary naked, so that everybody could see the "A-U-B-U-R-N" embossed on your chest, reading from top to bottom.

Moving right along, you get to the left-hand side and your wondering eyes fall upon four three-inch chrome-plated flexible tube exhaust pipes! Four gleaming pipes sweeping down and back large enough to carry away the exhaust from Krakatoa. Never mind that the poor convoluted exhaust manifold has to make all manner of tortured right-angle twists and turns before the pollutants can reach the shiny part and freedom. Never mind that the straight-eight Lycoming flathead has all it can do to crank out a hundred and fifty rather shortwinded horses. Those four pipes, all by themselves, are worth the twenty-two-forty-five price of admission. There's a big sign on the side of the hood, just above the louvers, that says "SUPER-CHARGED," but who needs it? Those four gleaming silver sewer pipes say it all.

Standing there, awed by the side elevation, you become aware of the cockpit. Framed by a sharply raked, vee-split windshield and very swoopy cutdown doors, the cockpit looks like a suitable venue for Captain Nemo, particularly if Captain Nemo happens to be on the slim side.

All the Auburn's exterior vastness is forgotten in the cockpit; it is cramped and uncomfortable. The steering wheel is large and it fits neatly against the old solar plexus. The door presses against your side and the space around the pedals is constricted. But whatever qualms you may have about the long-distance touring comfort of the Auburn interior are more than compensated for by the sheer feeling of quality exuded thereby. Everything is made of something solid, genuine, and reassuring. No "simulated look of wood grain," none of the disposable plastic trim that we all keep replacing on our modern automobiles. Just solid, durable stuff that was a lot of trouble to manufacture and install.

The instrument panel is the best part. Grouped in front of the driver, legible and handsome, is a full complement of instruments and switches. Oil pressure, water temperature, fuel level and amps to the left, with tachometer and switches for dash lights, head- and tail-lamps, throttle and choke surrounding the Auburn trademark in the center, and the speedometer to the right. On the passenger's side, the radio controls are mounted in a panel that replaces the glove box door of other Auburn models. The dash panel itself is satin chrome, very neatly and expensively trimmed in low-gloss black enamel. The radio controls, marked "Auburn-Crosley," are connected by long flexible cables to the radio set itself, which is mounted in the engine compartment. The Crosley heater is hung under the dash on the passenger's side with self-contained controls.

Centered in front of the passenger is a small plaque bearing the legend: "This certifies that this AUBURN AUTOMOBILE has been driven 100.2 miles per hour before shipment. (Signed) Ab Jenkins." All Auburn Speedsters carried such a dash plaque—with the claimed top speed invariably modestly over the ton—and it is said that either Ab Jenkins or Wade Morton really did drive each car and personally attest to its performance by scratching his name and the speed attained in the spaces provided. There's also some evidence to support the thesis that the plaques were phonies, just more of Cord's high-flying press agentry, but I for one prefer to believe that old Ab Jenkins hisself did in fact sit in that big yellow mother and hammer it down the road at "100.2 miles per hour before shipment."

Other goodies in the cockpit included the

control for the Columbia two-speed rear axle, located in the center of the steering wheel, next to the horn button, and the Startix automatic self-starter. The Columbia two-speed offered a choice of final drive ratios, "High" being 5.1-to-one and "Low" being 3.4-to-one, enabling the driver to cut engine revs by about a third when cruising in top. The two-speed axle could also be used as a passing gear, with the 5.1 ratio available for sudden acceleration when required. The unit was vacuum-operated from the intake manifold, and could only be actuated by depressing the clutch pedal (making it, in effect, a pre-selector). Lots of folks thought that the two-speed turned the less-than-delightful three-speed Warner transmission into a six-speed, but nobody in his right mind would try to use it that way. Nobody had the kind of coordination that would have been demanded by the clutch/shift lever/axle control choreography. Startix was an automatic self-starter that caused the engine to turn over as soon as the steering column-mounted ignition switch was turned on. And it would also restart the engine if it should happen to stall while driving. I love trick stuff like that.

Protecting all this was a disappearing canvas top. It's a good thing that it could be induced to disappear, too, because gorgeous it wasn't. If you have ever owned an English sports car, you will know something of the trials and tribulations involved in stowing the Auburn's top. If not, this passage from the owner's manual might cause you to thank God for the modern convertible top. To wit:

Lowering Speedster Top—Unhook the two curtain fasteners on each side of top. Unlock the deck lid, and reaching under lid from the front, unhook the eleven curtain hooks which are located at the rear underside of deck lid.

Pull back curtain up over deck lid. Open deck lid as far back as possible, lifting rear curtain in opening ahead of the opening lid.

Remove the three wing screws attaching front bow to windshield. Place second and third bows together in vertical position. Fold front bow back over second and third bows and down into deck lid opening so windshield grooves in front bow face rear of car.

Push second and third bows down into deck lid opening in vertical position. Open golf bag door and place right end of front bow through the door opening, then place left end of front bow down in deck lid opening and centralize bow by pulling it back from golf door opening. Fold second and third bows down on front bow and close golf bag door and deck lid.

To raise the top, reverse the procedure.

Behind the cockpit we have the famous Auburn Speedster's boat tail, which bears no resemblance whatsoever to any boat anybody ever saw. This particular boat tail doesn't look much like anything anybody ever saw. Inasmuch as automotive executives cannot visualize cars in any position but a three-quarter front view, it is possible that nobody at Auburn noticed or even cared that the car looked weird from the back. Seen from the official industry three-quarter front view, the way the tail of the car curves down and away is very nice. Seen from the rear it doesn't make any sense at all. Maybe that's why everybody loves it so. It is a true non-sequitur in automotive terms. Maybe old Gordon M. Buehrig, who designed it, just thought it was kind of a fun thing to do.

Driving the Speedster is not the same awe-

Although the cockpit is cramped and uncomfortable, it looks so good that you practically don't mind.

The Auburn Speedster's engine is hard pressed to crank out 150 horsepower, but the exhaust pipes look ample enough to carry away the fumes from Krakatoa.

inspiring experience as looking at it. It goes down the road like any other American car of the period, which is to say clumsily and without the slightest shred of agility or sportiness. But the car cannot be blamed for its failings in this area, it is a product of its environment. All American cars were pigs between the Depression and the Korean War, so why should the poor old Auburn have been any different? It is only that the car's appearance promises so much . . . so much that the mechanical underpinnings flatly refuse to deliver. A pity.

It was only a year or so after our buttercup-yellow Auburn first saw life that Mr. Errett Lobban Cord's automotive empire collapsed. By that time Mr. Cord had decamped with some very heavy bread and was incommunicado at his estate in England. The people of Auburn, Indiana, have never forgiven him, but they are too harsh. It is patently obvious that Auburn, Indiana, could never have become the automotive capital of the world anyway. For one thing, the commute from Hamtramick, Michigan, would have been too long. For another, America has never been very big on rewarding people who can take ordinary, undistinguished things and make them beautiful. When one compares Detroit's success with Indiana's failure, one is reminded of H.L. Mencken, who said, "Nobody ever lost money underestimating the taste of the American public."